The Hulton Getty Picture Coll

1920s

The Hulton Getty Picture Collection

1920s

Decades of the 20th Century
Dekaden des 20. Jahrhunderts
Décennies du XXe siècle

Nick Yapp

KÖNEMANN

First published in 1998 by Könemann Verlagsgesellschaft mbH, Bonner Straße 126, D-50968 Köln

This book was produced by The Hulton Getty Picture Collection Limited, Unique House, 21–31 Woodfield Road, London W9 2BA

For Könemann:
Production director: Detlev Schaper
Managing editor: Sally Bald
Project editor: Susanne Hergarden
Production assistant: Nicola Leurs
German translation: Angela Ritter
Contributing editor: Daniela Kumor
French translation: Francine Rey
Contributing editor: Stéphanie Aurin

For Hulton Getty:
Art director: Michael Rand
Design: Ian Denning
Managing editor: Annabel Else
Picture editor: Ali Khoja
Picture research: Alex Linghorn
Editor: James Hughes
Proof reader: Elisabeth Ihre
Scanning: Paul Wright, Andy Cockayne
Production: Robert Gray
Special thanks: Leon Meyer, Téa Aganovic and Antonia Hille

Typesetting by Greiner & Reichel Fotosatz. Colour separation by Saxon Photolitho Ltd.
Printed and bound by Sing Cheong Printing Co. Ltd., Hong Kong, China

ISBN 3-8290-0519-9

Frontispiece: 'Fashion is architecture; it is a matter of proportions'. The words are from Coco Chanel. The suit is from the Mattita Fashion House. The date is 1927.

Frontispiz: „Mode ist Architektur; sie ist eine Frage der Proportionen." Diese Worte stammen von Coco Chanel. Das abgebildete Kostüm ist eine Schöpfung des Modehauses Mattita aus dem Jahr 1927.

Frontispice : « La mode, c'est comme l'architecture. C'est une question de proportions. » Ces mots sont de Coco Chanel. L'ensemble est signé Mattita. On est en 1927.

Contents / Inhalt / Sommaire

Introduction

They called it the Jazz Age, but it was crazier than any of the razzmatazz that Jelly Roll Morton or Bix Beiderbecke produced. By 1929, when the bloated stock exchange on Wall Street so spectacularly crashed, the world had already turned itself upside down and inside out several times over. In the United States, Prohibition had created more drunks and more gangsters than legal drinking ever did. In Europe, the peace treaties of 1919 had soured international relations as bitterly as any war. In the Soviet Union, millions of new communists died so that the old order could be ploughed under. In Germany, people decorated their rooms with bank notes – it was cheaper than using wallpaper. And all over the world, victims of colonial power began to hope that the time was drawing nearer when their countries would be free and they could sweep aside their European masters.

After the horror and slaughter of World War I, few believed life could return to pre-war normality. As the decade unfolded, the General Strike, birth control, the Charleston, the radio, and Rudolph Valentino made sure it couldn't. As the decade continued, people became accustomed to the names of Hitler, Mussolini, Stalin, Hirohito, and others who were to come to a full terrifying significance in the Thirties.

In the arts, Isadora Duncan unchained the spirit of dance, but strangled to death on her own scarf in a tragic car accident. Surrealism and Dadaism flourished by rejecting established principles, and James Joyce became famous by rejecting established punctuation. Evelyn Waugh amused many, D H Lawrence shocked some. It was the era of George Gershwin and Irving Berlin, Igor Stravinsky and Arnold Schönberg, the lively flapper and the naughty 'New Woman', Oxford bags and raccoon coats, and it was the only time in history when it was smart to play the ukelele.

Across the world, sporting heroes included cricketer Jack Hobbs, tennis player Suzanne

Lenglen, footballer Dixie Dean, baseball player Babe Ruth, and Malcolm Campbell, holder of world records on land and water. George Mallory and Andrew Irvine trudged their way to within 800 feet (245 metres) of the summit of Everest, without the aid of oxygen, and may well have reached the top, but were never seen again.

Albert Einstein won the Nobel prize for Physics. Alexander Fleming discovered penicillin. Howard Carter and Lord Carnarvon opened up Tutankhamen's tomb to disturb the boy pharaoh who had lain in peace for thousands of years. Charles Lindbergh flew across the Atlantic in *The Spirit of St Louis*. The first 'talkies' thrilled millions of movie-goers. But it wasn't all progress. In Tennessee, a biology teacher was prosecuted for teaching the theory of evolution. The Ku Klux Klan burnt their torches and lynched the innocent in the Deep South. The United States legally, but wrongly, executed Sacco and Vanzetti. Leopold and Loeb gained their longed-for brief notoriety by strangling a 14-year-old boy.

There was death on the streets – in Ireland, where Republicans fought the Free Staters and the Black and Tans fought both; in Germany, where Freikorps and Spartacists warmed the weapons that the Nazis were soon to use more efficiently; in civil wars that stretched from Mexico to China; and in a beer warehouse in Chicago on St Valentine's Day in 1929.

Einführung

Man nannte es das Zeitalter des Jazz, aber tatsächlich war es noch verrückter als die Musik von Jelly Roll Morton oder Bix Beiderbecke. Bis zum New Yorker Börsensturz von 1929 war die Welt mehrfach aus den Angeln gehoben worden: In den Vereinigten Staaten hatte die Prohibition mehr Menschen in die Trunksucht und Kriminalität getrieben als zuvor, als Alkohol noch legal war. In Europa hatten die Friedensverträge von 1919 den internationalen Beziehungen ebensosehr geschadet wie jeder Krieg. In der Sowjetunion starben Millionen Kommunisten, damit die alte Ordnung begraben werden konnte. In Deutschland tapezierten die Menschen ihre Wohnungen mit Geldscheinen, weil sie weniger wert waren als Tapeten. Und überall auf der Welt begannen die Opfer der Kolonialmächte zu hoffen, daß ihre Länder bald von jeglicher europäischer Herrschaft befreit sein würden.

Nach dem Leid und Blutvergießen des Ersten Weltkrieges glaubten nur wenige Menschen, daß sie zu einem normalen Alltag zurückkehren konnten. Und dem war auch so, denn der Generalstreik in Großbritannien, die Geburtenkontrolle, der Charleston, das Radio und Rudolph Valentino verhinderten dies zu Beginn jenes Jahrzehnts. In dessen Verlauf gewöhnten sich die Menschen an Namen wie Hitler, Mussolini, Stalin und Hirohito und andere, die in den dreißiger Jahren eine grauenvolle Bedeutung erhalten sollten.

In der Welt der Künste befreite Isadora Duncan den Geist des Tanzes, erdrosselte sich jedoch mit dem eigenen Schal bei einem tragischen Autounfall. Der Surrealismus und der Dadaismus erlebten ihre Blütezeit, und James Joyce warf die traditionelle Zeichensetzung über Bord. Evelyn Waugh bereitete vielen Lesern Vergnügen, während D. H. Lawrence so manche schockierte. Es war das Zeitalter von George Gershwin und Irving Berlin, von Igor Strawinsky und Arnold Schönberg, von aufgeweckten, modebewußten Mädchen und der frechen „Neuen

Frau“, von weitgeschnittenen Hosen und Pelzmänteln aus Waschbärfell – und es war wohl die einzige Periode, in der es als schick galt, eine Ukulele zu spielen.

Zu den Sportgrößen gehörten der Kricketspieler Jack Hobbs, die Tennisspielerin Suzanne Lenglen, der Fußballspieler Dixie Dean, der Baseball-Crack Babe Ruth und Malcolm Campbell, der die Geschwindigkeitsweltrekorde zu Wasser und zu Lande hielt. George Mallory und Andrew Irvine bestiegen den Mount Everest und gelangten ohne Sauerstoffgeräte bis auf 245 Meter an den Gipfel heran. Ob sie ihn erreichten, ist unklar, denn sie wurden nie wieder gesehen.

Albert Einstein gewann den Nobelpreis für Physik, und Alexander Fleming entdeckte das Penicillin. Howard Carter und Lord Carnarvon öffneten die Grabstätte des jung verstorbenen Pharaos Tutenchamun, der jahrtausendelang in Frieden geruht hatte. Charles Lindbergh überquerte den Atlantischen Ozean in seinem Flugzeug *The Spirit of St. Louis*, und die ersten Tonfilme begeisterten Millionen von Kinobesuchern. Doch es gab nicht nur Fortschritte zu verzeichnen. In Tennessee wurde ein Biologielehrer strafrechtlich verfolgt, weil er im Unterricht die Evolutionstheorie behandelt hatte. Der Ku-Klux-Klan begann seinen Terror gegen Minderheiten und lynchte in den Südstaaten unschuldige Menschen. Die USA ließen Sacco und Vanzetti nach einem Fehlurteil hinrichten, und Leopold und Loeb erlangten mit dem Mord an einem 14jährigen Jungen eine kurze, traurige Berühmtheit.

Auf den Straßen lauerte der Tod – in Irland kämpften Republikaner gegen die Befürworter eines Freistaates und Braun- und Schwarzhemden gegen beide; in Deutschland griffen Freikorps und Spartakisten zu den Waffen, die die Nationalsozialisten bald sehr viel wirkungsvoller einsetzen sollten; Bürgerkriege tobten von Mexiko bis China, und in einem Chicagoer Lagerhaus für Bier wurde am Valentinstag im Jahre 1929 Blut vergossen.

Introduction

On l'appela l'âge du jazz, mais l'époque fut plus folle encore que la musique de Jelly Roll Morton ou de Bix Beiderbecke. En 1929, au moment de l'effondrement spectaculaire de la Bourse de New York, la face du monde avait déjà changé plusieurs fois. Aux Etats-Unis, la prohibition avait généré plus d'alcooliques et de gangsters que la période de consommation libre. En Europe, les traités de paix de 1919 avaient rendu les relations internationales aussi tendues qu'en temps de guerre. En Union soviétique, des millions de défenseurs du communisme mouraient pour en finir avec l'ordre ancien. En Allemagne, les gens recouvraient leurs murs de billets de banque – c'était moins cher que du papier peint. Un peu partout dans le monde, les opprimés des puissances coloniales se mirent à espérer que leurs pays seraient bientôt indépendants, libérés du joug des colons européens.

Après l'horreur et les massacres de la Première Guerre mondiale, peu de gens pensaient que la vie pourrait reprendre un cours normal. Au cours de la décennie, la grève générale de 1926, le contrôle des naissances, le charleston, la radio et Rudolph Valentino étaient autant de signes qu'il n'y aurait pas de retour en arrière. Les années passant, les gens s'accoutumaient aux noms de Hitler, Mussolini, Staline, Hirohito et de bien d'autres encore. Ce n'est que dans les années trente qu'ils seraient associés au pire.

Dans le monde des arts, Isadora Duncan sut libérer l'esprit de la danse avant de mourir tragiquement dans un accident de voiture, étranglée par sa propre écharpe. Le surréalisme et le dadaïsme fleurissaient, en défiant l'ordre établi, et James Joyce connut la célébrité en rejetant les règles de la ponctuation. Evelyn Waugh divertissait ses lecteurs tandis que D. H. Lawrence en choquait plus d'un. Ce fut l'époque de George Gershwin et Irving Berlin, Igor Stravinski et Arnold Schönberg, des filles délurées et de la « Femme Nouvelle », coquine, des pantalons très amples et des manteaux en raton laveur et aussi la seule époque où il était chic de jouer de la guitare hawaïenne.

Le monde du sport avait pour héros le joueur de cricket Jack Hobbs, la joueuse de tennis Suzanne Lenglen, le footballeur Dixie Dean, le joueur de baseball Babe Ruth, sans oublier Malcolm Campbell qui détenait les records de vitesse sur terre et sur l'eau. George Mallory et Andrew Irvine se lancèrent dans l'ascension de l'Everest et parvinrent à 245 mètres du sommet, sans oxygène. Peut-être atteignirent-ils leur but, on ne les revit jamais.

Albert Einstein reçut le prix Nobel de la physique. Alexander Fleming ouvrit la pénicilline. Howard Carter et Lord Carnarvon ouvrirent la tombe de Toutankhamon, le pharaon qui reposait là, en paix, depuis des milliers d'années. Charles Lindbergh traversa l'Atlantique à bord du *The Spirit of St. Louis*. Les premiers films parlants suscitèrent l'enthousiasme de millions de spectateurs. Mais il n'y eut pas seulement que des progrès. Dans le Tennessee, un instituteur fut poursuivi en justice pour avoir enseigné la théorie de l'évolution. Le Ku Klux Klan brûlait ses torches et lynchait des innocents dans les Etats du Sud. Le gouvernement américain condamna Sacco et Vanzetti à mort, en toute légalité mais à tort. Léopold et Loeb, en mal de célébrité, connurent une brève notoriété après avoir étranglé un garçon de 14 ans.

Dans les rues, on comptait les morts – en Irlande, où les Républicains s'opposaient aux partisans d'un Etat libre tandis que les Chemises noires et brunes réprimait les deux camps ; en Allemagne, où les Freikorps et les Spartakistes aiguisaient les armes dont les Nazis ne tarderaient pas à faire usage, et dans les guerres civiles – de la Chine au Mexique – ou encore dans l'attentat qui ensanglanta un entrepôt de bière à Chicago le jour de la Saint-Valentin, en 1929.

1. Movers and shakers
Spieler und Gegenspieler
Bouleversements

Hitler was already leader of the National Socialist German Workers' Party when this photograph (and those overleaf) were taken by Heinrich Hoffman in 1925. They show Hitler posing while listening to a recording of one of his speeches. Hitler ordered Hoffman to destroy the negatives, but Hoffman kept them.

Hitler war bereits Vorsitzender der Nationalsozialistischen Deutschen Arbeiterpartei, als Heinrich Hoffmann 1925 diese Aufnahme (und jene auf den folgenden Seiten) machte. Der Führer posierte mit der für ihn typischen Gestik, während eine seiner Reden vom Tonband ablief. Hitler hatte Hoffmann zwar befohlen, die Negative zu vernichten, doch Hoffmann behielt sie.

Ce cliché (et ceux des pages suivantes) furent pris par Heinrich Hoffman en 1925. Hitler, déjà à la tête du parti national-socialiste des travailleurs allemands, écoute en gesticulant l'enregistrement de l'un de ses discours. Hitler ordonna à Hoffman de détruire les négatifs mais ce dernier les conserva.

1. Movers and shakers
Spieler und Gegenspieler
Bouleversements

World War I swept the old order aside. Empires were destroyed, royal houses tottered and fell. The Tsar was dead, the Kaiser was in permanent exile, the Hapsburgs had made their final bow. A new breed of politicians moved into the spotlight: Lenin, Atatürk, Mussolini. They were men with visions that would change the world, not just their own corner of it. Not for them some democratic tinkling with the existing system. They believed in the imposition of the new, and they brought to the Twenties hope and horror in roughly equal amounts.

The battles between their rival ideologies were fought on the streets, in *putsch* and counter-*putsch*. Lenin lived just long enough to see the Bolshevik state resist foreign invasion and survive civil war. He was spared the experience of Stalin in full flow. In Italy, Mussolini marched to Rome and power. In France and Britain, whiskered old gentlemen with wing collars enjoyed a late summer in office.

It was still too early for some of the key players of the future to take centre stage. They waited in the wings, with varying degrees of patience. But they were not merely understudies. When their time came, they would rewrite not just their own roles, but the entire drama.

Der Erste Weltkrieg bedeutete das Ende der alten Ordnung. Weltreiche wurden zerstört und Königshäuser fielen. Der Zar war tot, der Kaiser befand sich im ständigen Exil, und auch die Habsburger mußten abtreten. Eine neue Garde von Politikern trat ins Rampenlicht: Lenin, Atatürk und Mussolini. Ihre politischen Visionen sollten nicht nur ihr eigenes Land, sondern die ganze Welt verändern. Sie glaubten nicht an einen Wandel auf demokratischem Wege, sondern daran, daß man dem Volk ein neues System aufzwingen müsse. So erfüllten sie die zwanziger Jahre in gleichem Maße mit Hoffnung und Schrecken.

Der Kampf zwischen den Anhängern der rivalisierenden Ideologien fand in den Straßen statt. Auf jeden Putsch folgte ein Gegenputsch. Lenin erlebte noch, wie sich der bolschewistische Staat der Invasion aus dem Ausland widersetzte und den Bürgerkrieg überstand. Es blieb ihm jedoch erspart, Stalin in voller Aktion zu erleben. In Italien marschierte Mussolini auf Rom und ergriff die Macht. In Frankreich und Großbritannien genossen die älteren Herren mit Backenbart und Stehkragen noch einmal eine goldene Zeit in ihrem Amt.

Für einige der zukünftigen Hauptakteure war die Zeit für den großen Auftritt noch nicht reif. Sie warteten mit mehr oder weniger Geduld hinter den Kulissen, obwohl sie mehr als nur die zweite Besetzung waren. Als ihre Zeit schließlich kam, sollten sie nicht nur ihre eigenen Rollen umschreiben, sondern das gesamte Stück.

La Première Guerre mondiale balaya l'ordre établi, signifiant la fin des grands Empires et la chute des familles royales déjà chancelantes. Le tsar était mort, le Kaiser dut s'exiler et les Habsbourg se retirèrent du devant de la scène. Une nouvelle race d'hommes politiques vit le jour : Lénine, Atatürk, Mussolini. Ces hommes avaient des visions qui allaient changer le monde et pas seulement leur propre pays. Pour eux, il s'agissait de modifier profondément le système existant, d'aller au-delà de quelques mesures démocratiques. Convaincus qu'il fallait employer la force pour imposer le nouveau régime, ils suscitèrent dans les années vingt autant l'espoir que la terreur.

Les batailles entre partisans d'idéologies rivales étaient livrées dans la rue, à coup de putschs et de contre-putschs. Lénine vécut assez longtemps pour voir le régime bolchevik résister à l'invasion étrangère et survivre à la guerre civile, mais n'assista plus à la dérive du stalinisme. En Italie, Mussolini entreprit sa marche sur Rome et accéda au pouvoir. En France et en Grande-Bretagne, le pouvoir était entre les mains de vieux gentlemen à favoris et à cols cassés, qui finissaient leur carrière politique paisiblement.

Il était encore trop tôt pour occuper le devant de la scène et les hommes-clés du futur attendaient dans l'antichambre du pouvoir, plus ou moins patiemment. Mais ils n'étaient pas de simples doublures. Quand leur tour viendrait, ce ne serait pas uniquement leur propre rôle, mais toute l'histoire, qui serait réécrite.

Cheaper than toys. Children use wads of money as building blocks during the German inflation crisis of 1923.

Preiswerter als Spielzeug. Kinder verwenden während der deutschen Inflation von 1923 Geldbündel als Bausteine.

Moins cher que des jouets. Des enfants utilisent des liasses de billets comme cubes de constructions pendant l'inflation de 1923 en Allemagne.

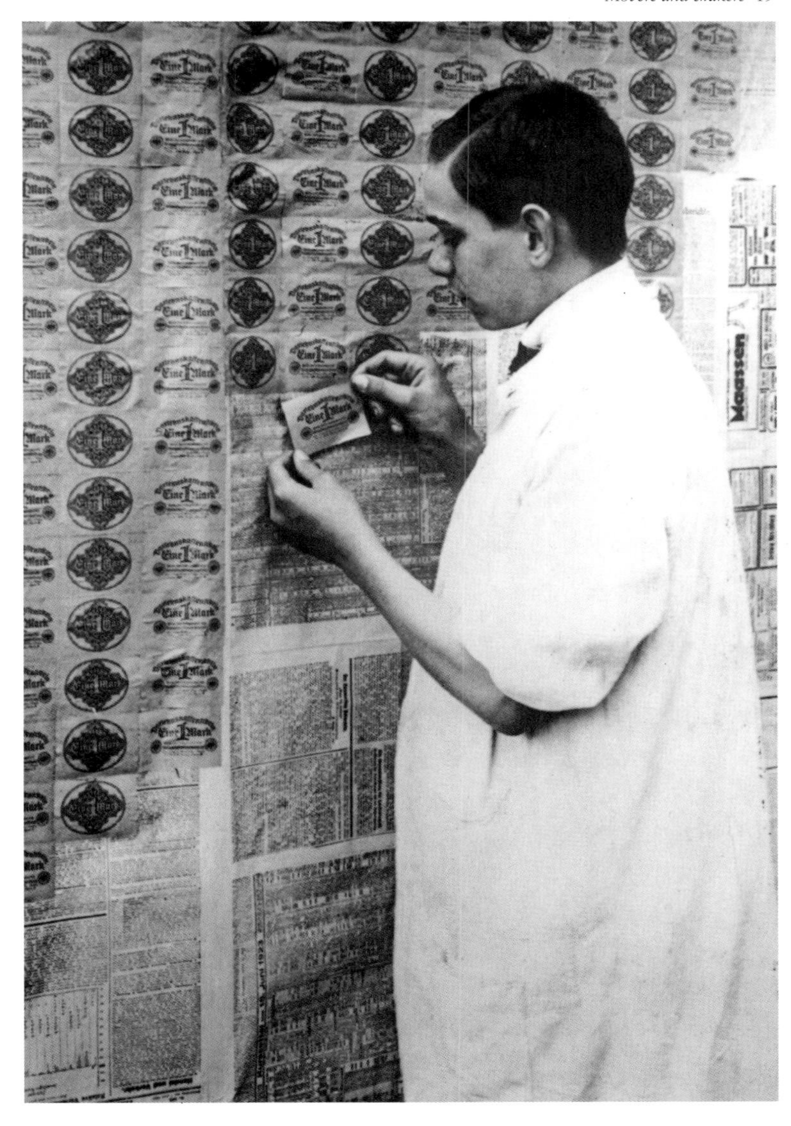

Cheaper than wallpaper. Bank notes decorate the walls of a German apartment. In one month, the reichsmark moved from 10,000 to the dollar, to 50,000.

Preiswerter als Tapete. Eine deutsche Wohnung wird mit Banknoten tapeziert. Innerhalb eines Monats verschlechterte sich der Kurs von 10.000 Reichsmark pro US-Dollar auf 50.000.

Moins cher que du papier peint. Des billets de banque allemands utilisés pour tapisser un appartement. En un mois, le reichsmark passa de 10 000 à 50 000 pour un dollar.

A group of Germans sabotage a railway locomotive near Düsseldorf during the crisis of 1923. 'All values were changed,' wrote Austrian writer and pacifist Stefan Zweig, '...The laws of the State were flouted, no tradition, no moral code was respected' – *The World of Yesterday*.

Bei Düsseldorf sabotieren einige Deutsche während der Krise von 1923 eine Lokomotive. „Alle Werte waren abhanden gekommen", schrieb der österreichische Schriftsteller und Pazifist Stefan Zweig, „... Die Gesetze des Staates wurden mißachtet und keine Tradition, kein Sittenkodex wurde mehr respektiert" – *Die Welt von Gestern*.

Des Allemands sabotent une locomotive près de Düsseldorf durant la crise de 1923. « Toutes les valeurs avaient changé », écrivait l'auteur et pacifiste autrichien Stefan Zweig dans *Le monde d'hier*, « ... les lois de l'Etat étaient bafouées, aucune tradition, aucun code moral n'était respecté ».

Germany, 1920. Dismantling a tank with a blowtorch. The harsh conditions of the Treaty of Versailles had included the banning of heavy weapons and the restriction of the German army to 100,000 men. There was talk of general disarmament, but it came to nothing.

Deutschland, 1920. Zerlegung eines Panzers mit Hilfe einer Lötlampe. Die strengen Bedingungen des Versailler Vertrages forderten unter anderem ein Verbot schwerer Artillerie und eine Beschränkung der Reichswehr auf 100.000 Soldaten. Eine generelle Abrüstung wurde ebenfalls erwogen, verlief jedoch später im Sande.

Allemagne, 1920. Démantèlement d'un tank à l'aide d'un chalumeau. Les clauses du traité de Versailles étaient sévères, interdisant, entre autres, toute artillerie lourde et limitant l'armée allemande à 100 000 hommes. Il avait été question de désarmement total mais il n'aboutit pas.

Swords into ploughshares, tanks into tractors. Soviet workers harness their plough to a British tank captured in the civil war, 1921. Britain and other Western countries sent thousands of troops to Murmansk in northern Russia, in an attempt to overthrow the Bolshevik government.

Schwerter werden zu Pflugscharen und Panzer zu Traktoren. Sowjetische Landarbeiter lassen ihren Pflug von einem britischen Panzer ziehen, den sie im russischen Bürgerkrieg eroberten, 1921. Großbritannien und andere westliche Nationen hatten damals versucht, die bolschewistische Regierung zu stürzen, und zu diesem Zweck Tausende von Soldaten ins nordrussische Murmansk entsandt.

Epées transformées en soc de charrue, tanks transformés en tracteurs. Des ouvriers soviétiques ont attaché une charrue à un tank britannique saisi pendant la guerre civile, 1921. La Grande-Bretagne et d'autres pays européens envoyèrent des milliers de soldats à Mourmansk, au nord de la Russie, dans le but de renverser le régime bolchevik.

From firepower to firewood. Workers cut up the wooden propellers of fighter planes that formed Germany's air force during World War I, to meet the terms of the Treaty of Versailles.

Feuerkraft wird zu Feuerholz. Gemäß den Bestimmungen des Versailler Vertrages werden hölzerne Propeller, die von deutschen Jagdflugzeugen des Ersten Weltkrieges stammen, zu Kleinholz verarbeitet.

Feu de tout bois. Des ouvriers scient les hélices en bois d'un avion de chasse de l'armée de l'air allemande ayant servi pendant la Première Guerre mondiale, conformément aux exigences du traité de Versailles.

New prophet.
Adolf Hitler reads a newspaper while in Landsberg Gaol, December 1924.
He served nine months of a five-year sentence.

Der neue Prophet.
Hitler beim Zeitunglesen im Gefängnis von Landsberg, Dezember 1924.
Von fünf Jahren verbüßte er lediglich neun Monate.

Nouveau prophète.
Adolf Hitler lisant un journal dans la prison de Landsberg, décembre 1924.
Condamné à une peine de cinq ans, il ne passa que neuf mois en prison.

1921. Old warriors. Aristide Briand, French prime minister (right), and war veteran Marshall Ferdinand Foch (left) visit British prime minister David Lloyd George at Chequers. Hitler described Lloyd George as 'the man who won the First World War'.

1921. Alte Krieger. Aristile Briand, Frankreichs Ministerpräsident (rechts), und der Kriegsveteran Marschall Ferdinand Foch (links) beim britischen Premierminister David Lloyd George in Chequers. Hitler bezeichnete Lloyd George als den „Mann, der den Ersten Weltkrieg gewann".

1921. Anciens combattants. Aristide Briand, le Premier ministre français (à droite), et le maréchal Foch, vétéran de la Grande Guerre (à gauche), chez le Premier ministre britannique David Lloyd George à Chequers. Pour Hitler, Lloyd George était « l'homme qui avait gagné la Première Guerre mondiale ».

Lloyd George and his daughter, Megan, on a visit to New York, 1923. Lloyd George's coalition government collapsed in 1922.

Lloyd George mit seiner Tochter Megan bei einem Besuch in New York, 1923. Die Koalitionsregierung unter Lloyd George war ein Jahr zuvor gescheïtert.

Llyod George et sa fille Megan, en visite à New York, 1923. Le gouvernement de coalition Lloyd fut dissous en 1922.

Aristide Briand, 1925. Briand was premier of France 11 times, won the Nobel Peace Prize in 1926, and founded the socialist newspaper *L'Humanité*.

Aristide Briand, 1925. Die Franzosen wählten Briand 11 Mal zum Regierungschef. Er gewann 1926 den Friedensnobelpreis und gründete die sozialistische Zeitung *L'Humanité*.

Aristide Briand, 1925. Onze fois président du Conseil, Briand reçut le prix Nobel de la paix en 1926. Il fonda également le jounal socialiste *L'Humanité*.

Unlikely bedfellows. Field Marshal Erich von Ludendorff (left) and Adolf Hitler, 1923. Ludendorff was the first Nazi candidate for president of the Reich.

Ein ungewöhnliches Gespann. Feldmarschall Erich von Ludendorff (links) und Adolf Hitler, 1923. Ludendorff war der erste nationalsozialistische Kandidat für das Amt des Reichspräsidenten.

Alliés de fortune. Le maréchal Erich von Ludendorff (à gauche) et Adolf Hitler, 1923. Ludendorff fut le premier candidat nazi à la présidence du Reich.

Plus-four pals. Edward, Prince of Wales, visits Prince Hirohito in Japan, August 1926. Later that year, Hirohito became emperor.

Knickerbocker-Freunde. Der Prinz von Wales, Edward, besucht Japan im August 1926 Prinz Hirohito, der noch im selben Jahr zum Kaiser gekrönt wurde.

Amis en culottes de golf. Le prince de Galles Edouard en visite chez le prince Hirohito au Japon, août 1926. Hirohito devint empereur la même année.

Success – the fascist March on Rome, 28 October 1922. Benito Mussolini (centre) leads the Black Shirts, flanked by Emilio de Bono (left) and Count Italo Balbo. De Bono opposed Mussolini in the Grand Fascist Council in 1943, and was executed. Balbo was killed when his plane was shot down in 1940.

Erfolg – der Marsch der Faschisten auf Rom, 28. Oktober 1922. Benito Mussolini (Mitte) führt die Schwarzhemden in Begleitung von Emilio de Bono (links) und Graf Italo Balbo. De Bono stellt sich 1943 im Großen Faschistischen Rat gegen Mussolini und wurde daraufhin exekutiert. Balbo war bereits 1940 bei einem Luftkampf ums Leben gekommen.

Victoire – la marche fasciste sur Rome, 28 octobre 1922. Benito Mussolini (centre) à la tête des Chemises noires, flanqué d'Emilio de Bono (à gauche) et du comte Italo Balbo. De Bono s'opposa à Mussolini au Grand conseil fasciste de 1943 et fut exécuté. Balbo mourut en 1940, son avion ayant été abattu.

Failure – Adolf Hitler (centre), Alfred Rosenberg (left), and Dr Friedrich Weber of the Freikorps Oberland (Free Corps), 9 November 1923. This was the day when the Nazis unsuccessfully attempted to overthrow the Bavarian government in Munich.

Mißerfolg – Adolf Hitler (Mitte), Alfred Rosenberg (links) und Dr. Friedrich Weber vom Freikorps Oberland am 9. November 1923. Es war der Tag, an dem der Putsch der Nationalsozialisten gegen die bayrische Regierung in München fehlschlug.

Echec – Adolf Hitler (centre), Alfred Rosenberg (à gauche) et le Dr Friedrich Weber des Freikorps Oberland (Corps francs), 9 novembre 1923. Ce jour-là à Munich, les nazis tentèrent sans succès de renverser le gouvernement bavarois.

A show of hands, Berlin, 1928. 80,000 Germans take an oath of allegiance to Hitler in the Lustgarten. The late Twenties saw an enormous growth in membership of the Nazi Party, from 17,000 to a million in just four years.

Handzeichen, Berlin, 1928. 80.000 Deutsche leisten Hitler im Lustgarten den Fahneneid. In den späten zwanziger Jahren hatte die NSDAP so starken Zulauf, daß sich die Mitgliederzahl innerhalb von nur vier Jahren von 17.000 auf eine Million erhöhte.

Salut nazi, Berlin, 1928. 80 000 Allemands prêtent serment à Hitler au Lustgarten. A la fin des années vingt, le nombre d'adhérents au parti national-socialiste passa en quatre ans de 17 000 à un million.

Rome, 1925. Mussolini in the grounds of the Villa Borghese. Il Duce was an enthusiastic sportsman, a talented ballroom dancer, and a melodramatic actor. The British diplomat Harold Nicholson described him as possessing 'showy vulgarity'.

Rom, 1925. Mussolini im Park der Villa Borghese. Il Duce war nicht nur ein begeisterter Sportler, sondern auch ein begabter Tänzer und melodramatischer Schauspieler. Der britische Diplomat Harold Nicholson empfand Mussolini allerdings als „theatralisch und vulgär".

Rome, 1925. Mussolini dans les jardins de la Villa Borghese. Le Duce était un grand sportif, un danseur accompli et un acteur mélodramatique. Selon le diplomate Harold Nicholson, il était d'« une vulgarité tapageuse ».

Right-wing cyclists salute Mussolini, November 1923. Mussolini's rise to power was breathtakingly fast. Within a few months of the March on Rome, he was in total control.

Rechtsgerichtete Radfahrer grüßen Mussolini, November 1923. Seine Machtergreifung gelang in atemberaubend kurzer Zeit. Bereits wenige Monate nach seinem Marsch auf Rom, war er der unumschränkte Herrscher Italiens.

Des cyclistes fascistes saluent Mussolini, novembre 1923. Mussolini accéda au pouvoir en un temps record. Quelques mois après « la marche sur Rome », il contrôlait tout le pays.

Germany, 1928. Newly-weds cut their wedding cake with an axe, while their guests make the fascist salute. The axe was a symbol of fascist power.

Deutschland, 1928. Ein junges Brautpaar schneidet die Hochzeitstorte mit einer Axt an, während die Gäste den Hitlergruß erbieten. Die Axt galt als ein Symbol faschistischer Macht.

Allemagne, 1928. Des jeunes mariés découpent le gâteau de mariage avec une hache tandis que les invités font le salut nazi. La hache était un symbole de puissance fasciste.

Berlin, 1920. Unskilled workers show their identity cards in an unemployment agency. In two months, the number of unemployed in the city trebled. On the outskirts there were gun battles over potato fields and farmers protected their crops with shotguns.

Berlin, 1920. Ungelernte Arbeiter zeigen in einer Stellenvermittlung ihre Ausweise. Innerhalb von zwei Monaten hatte sich die Zahl der Arbeitslosen in der Stadt verdreifacht. In der Umgebung gab es bewaffnete Auseinandersetzungen über den Besitz von Kartoffelfeldern und die Bauern verteidigten ihre Ernte mit Schrotflinten.

Berlin, 1920. Des ouvriers non qualifiés montrent leur carte d'identité dans une agence pour l'emploi. Le nombre de chômeurs tripla en deux mois dans la ville. Il y eut des affrontements armés dans les champs de pommes de terre autour de la ville, les fermiers protégeant leurs récoltes à coups de feu.

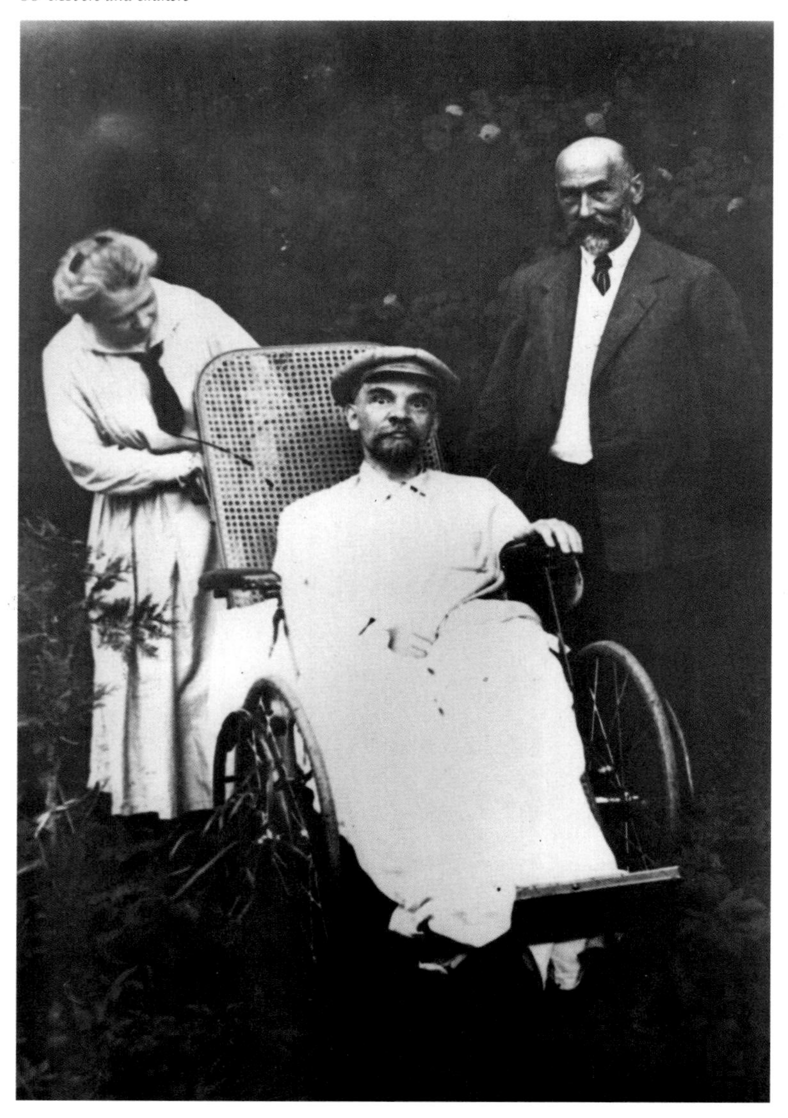

The last days of Lenin, 1923. After suffering a series of strokes, Lenin was nursed by his favourite younger sister, Maria Ulyanova.

Lenins letzte Tage, 1923. Nach mehreren Schlaganfällen pflegte ihn seine geliebte jüngere Schwester, Maria Uljanowa.

Les derniers jours de Lénine, 1923. Victime de plusieurs attaques, Lénine fut soigné par sa sœur cadette préférée, Maria Ulyanova.

Leon Trotsky, Russian Commissar for War, in the grounds of his villa at Sukham-Kale on the Black Sea, 1924 – the year of Lenin's death. Three years later, Trotsky was expelled from the Party by Stalin. In 1929 he was exiled.

Leo Trotzki, der russische Kriegskommissar, im Garten seiner Villa in Sukham-Kale am Schwarzen Meer, 1924 – Lenins Todesjahr. Drei Jahre später wurde Trotzki von Stalin aus der Partei ausgeschlossen. 1929 wurde er des Landes verwiesen.

Léon Trotski, commissaire russe à la Guerre, dans les jardins de sa villa à Sukham-Kale au bord de la mer Noire en 1924 – l'année de la mort de Lénine. Trois ans plus tard, Trotski fut expulsé du parti par Staline. En 1929, il fut exilé.

Josef Stalin (left) and his Commissar for Economy, Sergo Ordzhonikidze, shortly after Stalin had become Soviet leader in 1924.

Josef Stalin (links) mit seinem Wirtschaftskommissar Sergo Ordschonikidse, kurz nachdem Stalin 1924 die Führung des sowjetischen Staates übernommen hatte.

Joseph Staline (à gauche) et son commissaire à l'Economie, Serge Ordzhonikidze en 1924, peu de temps après avoir été élu chef du Parti.

Josef Stalin. For half a century rumours persisted that he was responsible for Lenin's death. He wasn't, but he seized power with almost irreverent speed.

Josef Stalin. Jahrzehntelang hielten sich Gerüchte, daß er für Lenins Tod verantwortlich gewesen sei. Dies entsprach zwar nicht der Wahrheit, doch hatte Stalin mit beinahe pietätloser Eile die Macht ergriffen.

Joseph Staline. Pendant un demi-siècle, des rumeurs circulèrent, imputant la mort de Lénine à Staline. C'était faux même si Staline, peu respecteux de son prédécesseur, prit le pouvoir sans attendre.

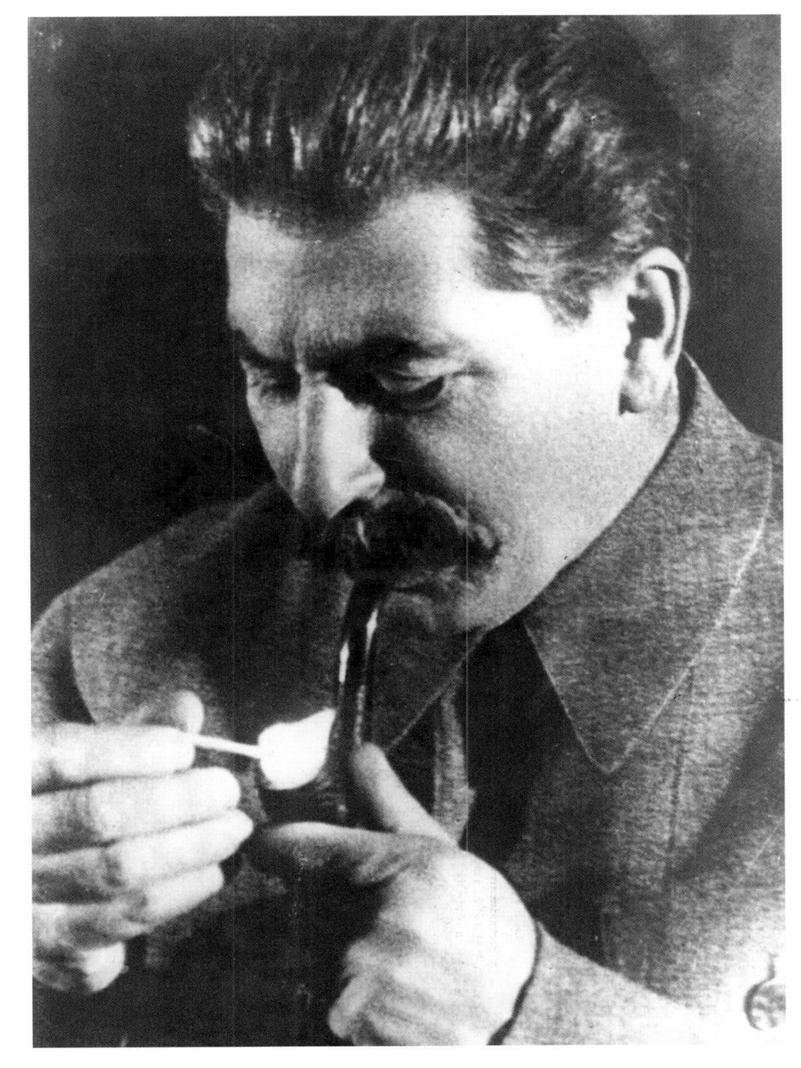

Bread and justice. Two petitioners (left) seek justice in the reception hall of Mikhail Ivanovich Kalinin, Chairman of the Soviets, Moscow, 1929. A starving child (right) in rural Russia during the civil war, 1921.

Brot und Gerechtigkeit. Zwei Bittsteller (links) bringen in der Empfangshalle des Vorsitzenden der Sowjets, Michail Iwanowitsch Kalinin, einen Rechtsstreit vor, Moskau, 1929. Ein verhungerndes Kind auf dem Land (rechts) während des Bürgerkriegs, 1921.

Pain et justice. Dans le hall d'entrée, deux pétitionnaires (à gauche) réclament justice auprès de Mikhaïl Ivanovitch Kalinine, président du Soviet suprême, Moscou, 1929. Enfant de la campagne russe (à droite), affamé durant la guerre civile, 1921.

Soviet fitness. Sportsmen and women march through Red Square, Moscow, 1927. Vast parades to promote physical culture were held twice a year, in November and May. The photograph is by Arkady Shaikhet.

Sowjetische Fitneß. Sportler und Sportlerinnen marschieren über den Roten Platz, Moskau, 1927. Im November und im Mai jedes Jahres fanden große Paraden statt, um die Körperkultur zu fördern. Die Aufnahme ist von Arkadi Schaichet.

Soviétiques en forme. Sportifs traversant la place Rouge, Moscou, 1927. De grands défilés avaient lieu deux fois par an, en novembre et en mai, pour promouvoir la culture physique. Cliché d'Arkady Shaikhet.

A group of German anti-fascists give the clenched fist salute in Berlin, September 1928. By that time, the communists viewed even the SPD (Social Democrats) as 'social fascists'.

Deutsche Antifaschisten entbieten den Arbeiterkampfgruß, Berlin, September 1928. Zu diesem Zeitpunkt betrachteten selbst die Kommunisten die SPD als eine Partei von „Sozialfaschisten".

Groupe d'antifascistes allemands, poings levés pour rendre leur salut, à Berlin, septembre 1928. A cette époque, les communistes considéraient que même le SPD (parti social-démocrate) était un parti de « fascistes sociaux ».

1922. The citizens of Vladivostok march in support of the Bolshevik Revolution. The Far Eastern Republic, of which Vladivostok was the capital, merged with Soviet Russia in November. Three years earlier it had been occupied by 70,000 Japanese troops supported by British and White Russian forces.

1922. Bürger von Wladiwostok unterstützten die bolschewistische Revolution mit einer Demonstration. Die fernöstliche Republik, deren Hauptstadt Wladiwostok war, vereinigte sich mit Sowjetrußland im November. Drei Jahre zuvor war sie mit der Unterstützung von britischen und weißrussischen Streitkräften von 70.000 japanischen Soldaten besetzt worden.

1922. Manifestation de soutien à la Révolution bolchevik à Vladivostok, capitale du territoire de Sibérie extrême-orientale qui adhéra à la Russie soviétique en novembre. Trois ans plus tôt, elle avait été occupée par 70 000 soldats japonais, soutenus par des forces britanniques et des Russes blancs.

London, 1928.
British communists celebrate May Day. By 1923 Lenin had already given up the idea of spontaneous communist risings in Western Europe. One can see why.

London, 1928.
Britische Kommunisten begehen den Maifeiertag. Diese Aufnahme zeigt, warum Lenin bereits um 1923 die Idee spontaner kommunistischer Aufstände in Westeuropa aufgegeben hatte.

Londres, 1928.
Des communistes britanniques célébrant le 1er Mai. En 1923 déjà, Lénine avait perdu tout espoir d'une révolution communiste spontanée en Europe de l'Ouest. On comprend pourquoi.

Occupied Germany. French troops on duty in Bochum during the occupation of the Ruhr, 1923. The French army advanced further into Germany in an attempt to force the payment of war reparations. Wilhelm Cuno, the German Chancellor, urged a policy of 'passive resistance'.

Besetztes Deutschland. Französische Soldaten in Bochum während der Besetzung des Ruhrgebiets, 1923. Die französische Armee rückte weiter in Deutschland vor, um die Zahlung von Kriegsreparationen zu erzwingen. Der deutsche Kanzler, Wilhelm Cuno, rief die Bevölkerung zum passiven Widerstand auf.

L'Allemagne occupée. Soldats français à Bochum durant l'occupation de la Ruhr, 1923. Des divisions françaises furent envoyées dans le centre du pays pour obtenir le paiement des réparations dues par les Allemands. Wilhelm Cuno, le chancelier allemand, décréta une « résistance passive ».

Occupied Ireland. Members of the Irish Republican Army patrol the streets of Dublin, July 1922. The IRA was violently opposed to the treaty that was negotiated between Britain and the Free Staters, led by Arthur Griffith and Michael Collins.

Besetztes Irland. Mitglieder der Irischen Republikanischen Armee patrouillieren durch die Straßen Dublin, 1922. Die IRA sprach sich entschieden gegen den Vertrag aus, der zwischen Großbritannien und den Befürwortern eines Freistaates unter der Führung von Arthur Griffith und Michael Collins ausgehandelt worden war.

L'Irlande occupée. Membres de l'Armée Républicaine Irlandaise en patrouille dans les rues de Dublin, juillet 1922. L'I. R. A. s'opposa violemment au traité que la Grande-Bretagne négocia avec les partisans de l'Etat libre, menés par Arthur Griffith et Michael Collins.

A new Turkey. Young Turks assemble to celebrate victory in Smyrna (Izmir), September 1922. The Turkish army under Mustafa Kemal Atatürk captured the city, and drove the Greeks out of Thrace. The victory was followed by scenes of looting and massacre.

Eine neue Türkei. Junge Türken versammeln sich zu einer Siegesfeier in Smyrna (Izmir), September 1922. Die türkische Armee unter Mustafa Kemal Atatürk hatte die Stadt eingenommen und die Griechen aus Thrakien vertrieben. Dem Sieg folgten Plünderungen und Massaker.

Une nouvelle Turquie. Jeunes Turcs célébrant la victoire à Smyrne (Izmir), septembre 1922. L'armée turque menée par Mustafa Kemal Atatürk conquit la ville et chassa les Grecs hors de la Thrace. La victoire fut suivie de pillages et de massacres.

Mustafa Kemal Atatürk, President of the Turkish Republic, 1924. From 1909 he led the Turkish Nationalist Movement, and took over the country when the Ottoman empire collapsed.

Mustafa Kemal Atatürk, der Präsident der türkischen Republik, 1924. Er leitete die Türkische Nationale Bewegung bereits seit 1909 und übernahm die Führung des Landes, als das Osmanische Reich zusammenbrach.

Mustafa Kemal Atatürk, président de la République turque, 1924. A la tête du mouvement nationaliste turc dès 1909, il accéda au pouvoir après l'effondrement de l'Empire ottoman.

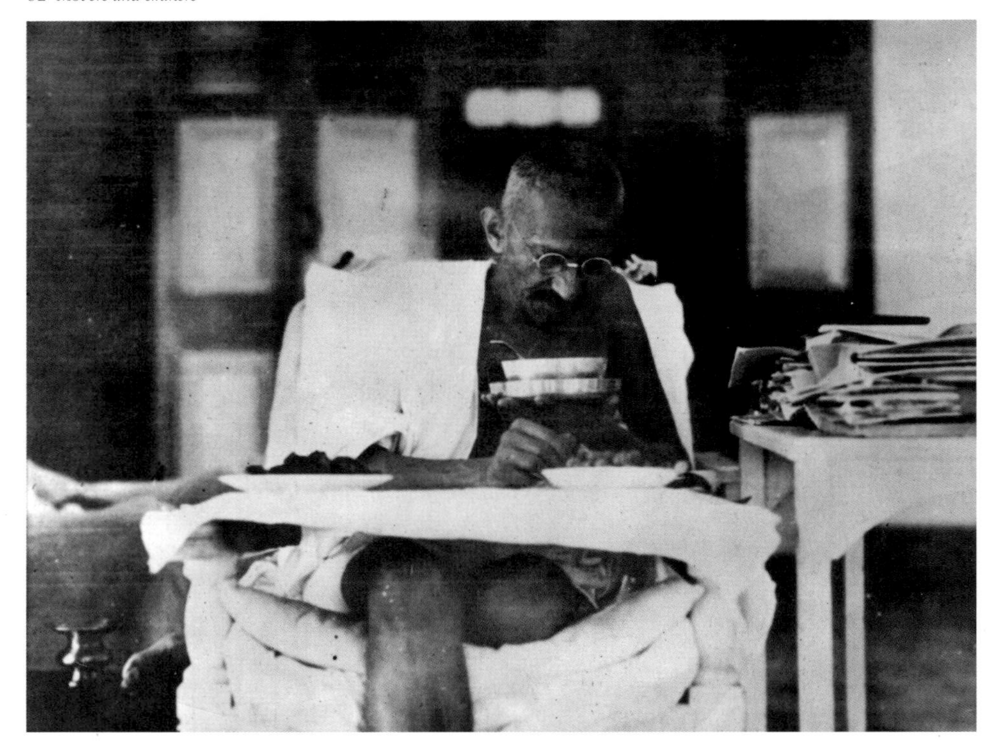

May 1924. Mohandas Gandhi at home, after his release from gaol. When sentencing Gandhi, Justice Broomfield remarked, 'If the course of events should make it possible for the Government to reduce the sentence, no one will be better pleased than I.'

Mai 1924. Mahatma Gandhi zu Hause, nach seiner Entlassung aus dem Gefängnis. Richter Broomfield bemerkte bei Gandhis Verurteilung: „Wenn der Lauf der Dinge es der Regierung ermöglichen sollte, das Urteil zu mildern, dann wäre darüber niemand glücklicher als ich."

Mai 1924. Mahatma Gandhi chez lui, après sa sortie de prison. Au procès, le juge Broomfield déclara à Gandhi que « si cela était possible au gouvernement de réduire la peine, personne ne serait plus heureux que moi. »

Gandhi addresses employees of the Tata Iron Works in Jamshedpur, near Calcutta, 1925. At this time, Lord Birkenhead, Secretary of State for India, announced, 'It is perfectly inconceivable that India will ever be fit for Dominion self-government.'

Gandhi spricht zur Arbeiterschaft der Eisenhütte Tata in Jamshedpur bei Kalkutta, 1925. Der für Indien zuständige britische Minister, Lord Birkenhead, erklärte damals: „Es ist völlig undenkbar, daß Indien jemals in der Lage sein wird, sich als Dominion selbst zu verwalten."

Gandhi s'adressant aux ouvriers de l'usine sidérurgique Tata s à Jamshedpur, près de Calcutta, 1925. A cette époque, lord Birkenhead, secrétaire d'Etat pour l'Inde, déclara qu'« il était absolument impensable que l'Inde acquière un jour le statut de dominion autonome ».

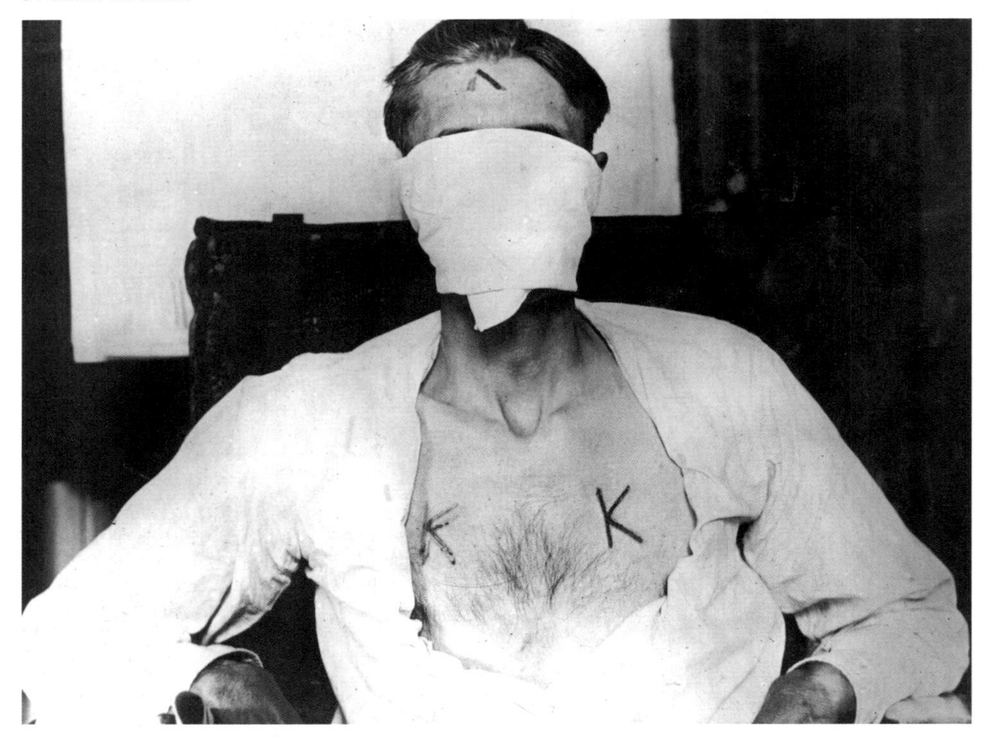

Scars of intolerance – a victim of the Klan. Nelson Burroughs refused to renounce his Roman Catholic beliefs and was branded by members of the Ku Klux Klan in the United States in 1924.

Narben der Intoleranz – ein Opfer des Ku-Klux-Klan. Weil Nelson Burroughs seinem römisch-katholischen Glauben nicht abschwören wollte, wurde er 1924 von Mitgliedern des Ku-Klux-Klan in den Vereinigten Staaten gebrandmarkt.

Marques de l'intolérance – victime du Klan. Pour n'avoir pas renoncé à ses croyances catholiques, Nelson Burroughs fut marqué aux fers par le Ku Klux Klan aux Etats-Unis, 1924.

Symbol of hatred. The Fiery Cross burns above a parade of Klansmen, August 1925.

Symbol des Hasses. Ein Flammenkreuz lodert über den Teilnehmern eines Aufmarsches des Ku-Klux-Klan, August 1925.

Symbole de haine. Croix de feu surplombant une procession du Ku Klux Klan, août 1925.

2. Haves and have-nots
Arm und Reich
Les nantis et les démunis

The classic day out, June 1922. 'Toffs' watch the Derby from the roof of their car, Epsom racecourse. There was clearly no room for the chauffeur. The race was won by Captain Cuttle, ridden by Steve Donaghue.

Ein klassischer Ausflug, Juni 1922. Vornehme Herrschaften verfolgen das Derby von Epsom vom Wagendach aus. Natürlich gab es keinen Platz mehr für den Chauffeur. Das Rennen gewann Steve Donaghue auf Captain Cuttle.

Une excursion typique, juin 1922. Des « aristos » assistent au Derby d'Epsom, perchés sur le toit de leur voiture. Le chauffeur n'a pas été invité à les rejoindre. Captain Cuttle, monté par Steve Donaghue, gagna la course.

2. Haves and have-nots
Arm und Reich
Les nantis et les démunis

For dukes and counts and grandees, the writing was already on the wall in the Twenties. Good breeding was no longer synonymous with a healthy bank balance. American millionaires were infiltrating the finest families in the Western world by means of their well-heeled daughters. And if his lordship couldn't obtain a young heiress, then he had to sell an old master.

For the masses, the decline of the aristocrat and the rise of the parvenu made little difference. They were still crammed into overcrowded tenements or dingy back-to-back houses. They smoked cheap tobacco, ate adulterated food and prayed to keep their jobs.

Rich and poor occasionally met, sometimes clashed, but the social structure and the social calendar remained largely unchallenged. There were the hunting, shooting and fishing seasons, presentations at Court, elegant balls and 12-course banquets. The finest houses in any city were still the private homes of titled individuals, not the offices of public corporations.

The shock waves of the Bolshevik Revolution were beginning to recede. Apoplectic colonels still wrote letters to the *Times* recommending ways of 'countering the red menace', but the threat of world revolution never materialized.

And so, although the writing was on the wall, the dance went on...

Für Herzöge, Grafen und andere hohe Herrschaften standen die Zeichen in den zwanziger Jahren auf Veränderung. Eine gute Kinderstube war nicht mehr mit einem vollen Konto gleichzusetzen. Amerikanische Millionäre verschafften sich Einlaß in die besten Familien, indem ihre Töchter eine großzügige Mitgift mitbrachten. Und wenn seine Lordschaft keine junge Erbin gewinnen konnte, so mußte er eben einen alten Meister versetzen.

Für die Massen machte der Untergang der Aristokraten und der Aufstieg der Neureichen kaum einen Unterschied. Sie lebten immer noch zusammengepfercht in überfüllten und oft schmuddeligen Mietshäusern, eines neben dem anderen. Sie rauchten billigen Tabak, verzehrten verdorbenes Essen, und beteten, daß ihnen der Arbeitsplatz erhalten blieb.

Arm und Reich trafen gelegentlich aufeinander, kollidierten mitunter, doch die soziale Struktur und die gesellschaftlichen Zusammenkünfte blieben größtenteils bestehen. Es gab noch immer die Jagd- und Angelsaison, Zeremonien bei Hof, elegante Bälle und Bankette mit 12 Gängen. Die schönsten Häuser der Stadt gehörten noch immer dem Adel und waren nicht etwa Bürohäuser staatlicher Unternehmen.

Die Erschütterungen, die die bolschewistische Revolution ausgelöst hatte, begannen allmählich abzuebben. Zwar schrieben auch weiterhin wütende Militärangehörige Leserbriefe an die *Times*, in denen sie Ratschläge erteilten, wie „der Roten Gefahr zu begegnen" sei – doch die Idee einer weltweiten Revolution verlief im Sande.

Und so wurde, obwohl das gesellschaftliche Barometer auf Sturm stand, weitergetanzt...

Pour les ducs, comtes et autres aristocrates, les signes d'un changement furent perceptibles dès les années vingt. Il ne suffisait plus d'être bien né pour avoir un compte en banque bien garni. Les millionnaires américains s'introduisaient dans les grandes familles d'Europe grâce à leurs filles richement dotées. Et si un lord manquait de moyens pour épouser une jeune héritière, il en était réduit à vendre un de ses vieux tableaux de maître.

Pour les masses, le déclin de l'aristocratie et l'émergence des nouveaux riches ne changèrent pas grand-chose. Elles continuaient à vivre dans des logements surpeuplés ou des maisons insalubres, alignées les unes contre les autres. Elles fumaient du tabac bon marché, mangeaient de la nourriture avariée et priaient pour ne pas perdre leur emploi.

Riches et pauvres se rencontrèrent et parfois s'affrontèrent mais les structures sociales et le calendrier mondain étaient inébranlables. Il y avait la chasse, le tir et la pêche, les visites à la Cour, les bals élégants et les banquets à 12 plats. En ville, les plus belles demeures n'avaient pas été encore transformées en bureaux et appartenaient toujours aux aristocrates.

L'onde de choc créée par la révolution bolchevik commençait à s'atténuer. Il y avait bien encore des colonels déchaînés pour écrire au *Times* et expliquer comment « contrer la menace rouge », mais le risque d'une révolution mondiale ne se matérialisa jamais.

Et même si les signes d'un changement étaient perceptibles, on continua à danser...

A beggar pursues a carriage across Epsom Downs on Derby Day, 1920. This is no ordinary carriage; seated in it (centre) is King George V. History, sadly, does not record whether the beggar had any luck.

Ein Bettler verfolgt hartnäckig eine Kutsche über die Epsom Downs am Tag des Derbys, 1920. Es ist keine gewöhnliche Kutsche, denn in ihr sitzt König Georg V. (Mitte). Leider ist nicht überliefert, ob der Einsatz des Bettlers erfolgreich war.

Un mendiant poursuit un fiacre se rendant au Derby d'Epsom, 1920. Ce n'est pas n'importe quel fiacre puisqu'il transporte le roi George V (au centre). Malheureusement, l'histoire ne dit pas si le mendiant eut de la chance ce jour-là.

At the bottom end of the market – a family huddle together in a slum tenement, Lisburn Street, Bethnal Green, East London, 1923.

Am unteren Ende des Wohnungsmarktes – eine Familie in einem Elendsquartier in der Lisburn Street im Ost-Londoner Stadtteil Bethnal Green, 1923.

Chez les plus démunis – famille habitant Lisburn Street à Bethnal Green, un quartier pauvre de l'est de Londres, 1923.

Dr Gornell (left) visits the Shadwell slums in the East End of London. Gornell worked for Dr Barnardo's, a charity that cared for orphaned, homeless or otherwise deprived working-class children.

Dr. Gornell (links) besucht die Slums von Shadwell im Londoner East End. Gornell war ein Mitarbeiter von Dr. Barnardo's, einer karitativen Organisation, die sich um verwaiste, obdachlose und anderweitig benachteiligte Kinder der Arbeiterklasse kümmerte.

Le Dr. Gornell (à gauche) en visite dans les taudis de Shadwell, un quartier de l'est de Londres. Il travaillait pour l'association Dr. Barnardo's, une institution charitable pour orphelins et enfants démunis ou sans abri provenant de la classe ouvrière.

'No place like home...' Families are housed in a disused prison, Worcester, 1926. The boast of many governments after World War I was that they would build 'homes fit for heroes'. For a while the intention was there, but somehow the will wasn't.

„Zu Hause ist es am schönsten ..." Diese Familien werden in einem leerstehenden Gefängnis in Worcester untergebracht, 1926. Viele Regierungen prahlten nach dem Ersten Weltkrieg damit, daß sie „Heime für Helden" bauen würden. Doch es blieb bei diesem Vorsatz.

« Rien ne vaut son chez soi... » Des familles sont logées dans une prison désaffectée, Worcester, 1926. Après la Première Guerre mondiale, bien des gouvernements promirent la construction « de logements dignes de leurs héros ». Ces bonnes intentions restèrent souvent sans effet.

A room with a view. Boxes at the Athens opera house are converted into living quarters during a serious housing shortage, 1925. The war with Turkey had made many Greeks homeless.

Zimmer mit Aussicht. Logen des Athener Opernhauses werden während einer großen Wohnungsnot in Unterkünfte verwandelt, 1925. Durch den Krieg mit der Türkei hatten viele Griechen ihr Heim verloren.

Chambre avec vue. Des loges de l'opéra d'Athènes transformées en habitations durant une sévère crise du logement, 1925. La guerre contre la Turquie laissa beaucoup de Grecs sans toit.

A pigsty becomes home for a family in Woking, England, 1921. That year a European economic crisis led to the withdrawal of house-building programmes.

Ein Schweinestall wird zum Einfamilienhaus umfunktioniert, Woking, England, 1921. In jenem Jahr führte die europäische Wirtschaftskrise zur Streichung von Wohnungsbauprogrammen.

Installation d'une famille dans une porcherie à Woking, Angleterre, 1921. Cette année-là, la crise économique qui sévit en Europe entraîna le retrait des programmes de construction de nouveaux logements.

The Daily Bread Institute, Bucharest, 1920. The defeat and collapse of the Austro-Hungarian empire at the end of World War I led to widespread chaos and poverty.

Tägliche Armenspeisung, Bukarest, 1920. Nach dem Ende des Ersten Weltkrieges und der erlittenen Niederlage stürzte der Zusammenbruch des österreichisch-ungarischen Kaiserreiches das Land in Chaos und Armut.

Centre de distribution de repas, Bucarest, 1920. La défaite et la chute de l'Empire austro-hongrois à la fin de la Première Guerre mondiale semèrent le chaos et la pauvreté.

The interior of a New York mission, with benches for beds, 1928. The slogans on the wall emphasizing religious and moral themes seem to fall on deaf ears.

In einer New Yorker Mission dienen Sitzbänke als Schlafstätten, 1928. Die religiösen und moralischen Sprüche der Wandplakate scheinen wohl auf taube Ohren zu stoßen.

Une mission de New York, avec des bancs comme lits, 1928. Les slogans religieux et moraux affichés au mur ne semblent pas troubler le sommeil de ces hommes.

'I like work. It fascinates me. I can look at it for hours' – Jerome K Jerome, *Three Men in a Boat*. Top-hatted gentry watch farm workers labouring in a field, 1925. In livelier times, the top hats would have been the rightful targets for clods of earth.

„Ich liebe die Arbeit. Sie fasziniert mich. Ich könnte stundenlang zusehen", schreibt Jerome K. Jerome in *Drei Mann in einem Boot*. Vornehme Herren mit Zylindern sehen Landarbeitern bei der Feldarbeit zu, 1925. In unruhigeren Zeiten wären die Zylinder sicher Zielscheibe für Erdklumpen gewesen.

« J'aime le travail. Il me fascine. Je peux le contempler des heures durant », Jerome K. Jerome dans *Trois Hommes dans un bateau*. Des aristocrates regardent des ouvriers agricoles labourer un champ, 1925. A des époques plus mouvementées, ces hauts-de-forme auraient été la cible idéale de mottes de terre.

Trainee fashion mannequins at a school of modelling and deportment in the West End of London, 1925. Balancing books on the head was thought to promote a straight back, a firm neck, and good posture. Balancing on one leg simply added to the challenge.

Mannequin-Ausbildung in einer Schule im Londoner West End, 1925. Das Balancieren eines Buches auf dem Kopf sollte einen geraden Rücken, einen festen Nacken und eine gute Haltung bewirken. Dabei auf einem Bein zu stehen war noch eine zusätzliche Herausforderung.

Exercice dans une école de mannequins et de maintien dans le West End de Londres, 1925. Marcher avec un livre sur la tête est idéal, paraît-il, pour se tenir droite sans fléchir la nuque. Garder l'équilibre sur un pied est encore plus périlleux.

1926. Members of the Monocle Club on a day out in the English countryside. The monocle was still fashionable in the Twenties, especially among inane young gentlemen and retired colonels.

1926. Mitglieder des Monokelvereins bei einem Ausflug aufs englische Land. Das Monokel war in den zwanziger Jahren noch immer in Mode, insbesondere bei einfältigen jungen Herren und pensionierten Militärangehörigen.

1926. Membres du Club du monocle, en excursion dans la campagne anglaise. Le monocle était encore à la mode dans les années vingt, surtout auprès des jeunes gens un peu niais et des colonels à la retraite.

London, 1926. The hunt comes to Oxford Street. The absence of traffic suggests that this photograph was taken early in the morning, on a Sunday, or possibly during the General Strike. Hyde Park was only a short canter away. The nearest fox was on Hampstead Heath.

London, 1926. Eine Jagdgesellschaft in der Oxford Street. Die verkehrslose Straße läßt vermuten, daß diese Aufnahme frühmorgens, an einem Sonntag oder möglicherweise während des Generalstreiks entstand. Der Hyde Park war nur einen kurzen Handgalopp entfernt. Dem nächsten Fuchs würde man allerdings erst auf Hampstead Heath begegnen.

Londres, 1926. Partie de chasse dans la Oxford Street. L'absence de voitures suggère que ce cliché fut pris très tôt le matin, un dimanche peut-être, pendant la grève générale. Hyde Park n'était qu'à quelques trots de là et le premier renard à Hampstead Heath.

A flock of 600 sheep is herded along Piccadilly, from Hyde Park to Green Park, London. This picture was taken at six o'clock in the morning.

Eine Herde von 600 Schafen wird in den Piccadilly zwischen Hyde Park und Green Park entlanggetrieben, London. Diese Aufnahme entstand um sechs um morgens.

Un troupeau de 600 moutons est emmené de Green Park à Hyde Park en passant par Piccadilly, Londres. Cette photographie fut prise à six heures du matin.

August 1928. The yacht *White Heather* sweeps along the Solent under full sail during the Royal Regatta at Cowes, Isle of Wight. Cowes Week was part of the Season's great sporting occasions.

August 1928. Die Segelyacht *White Heather* gleitet während der Königlichen Regatta von Cowes mit vollen Segeln den Solent entlang, Isle of Wight. Sie war eines der großen sportlichen Ereignisse der Saison.

Août 1928. Le *White Heather* glisse majestueusement, toutes voiles dehors, sur le détroit de Solent, île de Wight. Ce yacht participe à la semaine des Régates royales de Cowes, un des grands événements sportifs de la saison.

8
K 14

Barrel bath, 1925. The vast majority of houses were without bathrooms in the Twenties, though this method of keeping clean was exceptional.

Ein Bad in der Regentonne, 1925. Obwohl die meisten Häuser in den zwanziger Jahren kein Badezimmer besaßen, war die abgebildete Art der Körperhygiene wohl eher die Ausnahme.

Bain dans un tonneau, 1925. Dans les années vingt, rares étaient les maisons disposant d'une salle de bains. L'usage du tonneau pour se laver était néanmoins exceptionnel.

Battleship bath, 1920. Edward, Prince of Wales, and his cousin, Lord Louis Mountbatten, relax in a canvas swimming pool on board HMS *Renown*.

Ein Bad im Schlachtschiff, 1920. Der Prinz von Wales, Edward, entspannt sich mit seinem Cousin Lord Louis Mountbatten in einem Schwimmbecken aus Segeltuch an Bord der HMS *Renown*.

Bain sur un bateau de guerre, 1920. Le prince de Galles Edouard et son cousin, Lord Louis Mountbatten, se détendent dans une piscine en toile aménagée sur le paquebot HMS *Renown*.

Whitechapel locals enjoy dishes of jellied eels in the East End of London, September 1927. For many working-class gourmets, jellied eels were a special Sunday morning treat.

Einwohner des Stadtteils Whitechapel verzehren den begehrten Aal in Aspik, Londoner East End, September 1927. Für viele Feinschmecker der Arbeiterklasse waren Aale in Aspik am Sonntagmorgen ein besonderer Leckerbissen.

Des habitants de Whitechapel ravis de déguster des anguilles en gelée, un quartier de l'est de Londres, septembre 1927. Ce plat était, pour beaucoup d'ouvriers gourmets, un régal qu'ils pouvaient s'offrir uniquement le dimanche matin.

Every morning treat – Southwark schoolboys enjoy bottles of milk, October 1928. The provision of free milk to schoolchildren lasted until the Seventies in Britain. It was then ended by Margaret Thatcher.

Allmorgendlicher Genuß – Schüler aus Southwark trinken ihre Schulmilch, Oktober 1928. Die kostenlose Ausgabe von Milch an Schulkinder war in Großbritannien bis zum Beginn der Ära Thatcher in den siebziger Jahren üblich.

Dégustation quotidienne – des élèves de Southwark, ravis de boire leur bouteille de lait, octobre 1928. La distribution gratuite de lait dans les écoles britanniques se perpétua jusque dans les années soixante-dix. Margaret Thatcher mit alors fin à cette tradition.

Cold Turkey. Customers choose their turkeys from the display outside C C Hopkins' poultry shop in the City of London, Christmas 1929.

Kalter Truthahn. Bürger kaufen ihre Truthähne unter freiem Himmel vor C. C. Hopkins' Laden in der Londoner City, Weihnachten, 1929.

Viande froide. Les clients font leur choix de dinde devant l'étalage de C. C. Hopkins, marchand de volailles de la City à Londres, Noël 1929.

A bar in the City of London, December 1923. Many pubs ran Christmas clubs, where regular customers paid small sums of money throughout the year to buy a goose or turkey at Christmas time.

Eine Bar in der Londoner Innenstadt, Dezember 1923. In vielen Pubs gab es eine Weihnachtskasse, in die Stammgäste das ganze Jahr über kleinere Geldbeträge einzahlen konnten, um zur Weihnachtszeit eine Gans oder einen Truthahn zu erstehen.

Bar de la City à Londres, décembre 1923. Beaucoup de pubs tenaient une cagnotte de Noël. Les habitués y versaient des petites sommes d'argent tout au long de l'année et pouvaient ainsi s'acheter une dinde ou une oie à Noël.

January 1929.
A woman buys a snack from a coin-operated vending machine on Paddington Station, London.

Januar 1929.
Eine Frau zieht sich an einem Automaten im Londoner Bahnhof Paddington einen Imbiß.

Janvier 1929.
Une femme s'achète un en-cas au distributeur automatique de la gare de Paddington, Londres.

December 1926. Disabled ex-servicemen take tea in a Coventry café. By the end of World War I there were millions of severely wounded veterans of the war in Europe and the United States.

Dezember 1926. Versehrte Kriegsveteranen beim Tee in einem Café in Coventry. Am Ende des Ersten Weltkrieges gab es in Europa und den Vereinigten Staaten Millionen schwerbeschädigter Veteranen.

Décembre 1926. Des mutilés de guerre prennent leur thé dans un café de Coventry. Au lendemain de la Première Guerre mondiale, le nombre de vétérans gravement blessés se comptait par millions en Europe et aux Etats-Unis.

Childish amusement, January 1928. 950 naval cadets queue to see a performance of the pantomime *Dick Whittington* at the Elephant and Castle Theatre, London.

Vergnügen für jung und alt, Januar 1928. 950 Kadetten stehen vor dem Londoner Elephant and Castle Theatre Schlange, um eine Aufführung des Weihnachtsmärchens *Dick Whittington* zu sehen.

Divertissement enfantin, janvier 1928. 950 matelots font la queue pour assister au spectacle de pantomime intitulé *Dick Whittington*, donné à l'Elephant and Castle Theatre, Londres.

Amusing the children, 1921. J M Barrie (centre) joins the queue at a London coffee stall. Barrie is best known as the creator of *Peter Pan*, but in 1920 he wrote another fairytale play called *Mary Rose*.

Kinderträume, 1921. J. M. Barrie (Mitte) in der Schlange eines Londoner Kaffeestands. Barrie ist bekannt als Schöpfer von *Peter Pan*. 1920 schrieb er jedoch ein weiteres Märchenstück mit dem Titel *Mary Rose*.

Divertir les enfants, 1921. J. M. Barrie (au centre) devant une buvette à Londres. Barrie est surtout connu pour avoir écrit *Peter Pan* mais, en 1920, il écrivit un autre conte de fées intitulé *Mary Rose*.

August 1924. A newly-wed couple pose with their cockatoo. The bride's wedding dress is the height of Twenties style, a cheaper version of that worn by Lady Elizabeth Bowes-Lyon when she married the future King George VI, in April 1923.

August 1924. Ein frischvermähltes Paar posiert mit seinem Kakadu. Das Hochzeitskleid der Braut entspricht der elegantesten Mode der zwanziger Jahre und war eine weniger kostspielige Version des Kleides, das Lady Elizabeth Bowes-Lyon trug, als sie im April 1923 mit dem zukünftigen König Georg VI. vor den Traualtar trat.

Août 1924. Un couple de jeunes mariés pose avec son cacatoès. La robe de la mariée est du dernier cri. C'est une copie, moins chère, de la robe que portait lady Elizabeth Bowes-Lyon quand elle épousa le futur roi George VI en avril 1923.

The wedding game, February 1922. Children recreate the marriage of Princess Mary, daughter of King George V, to the Earl of Harewood. This was the first royal wedding to be broadcast to the nation, and became a popular children's game.

Das Hochzeitsspiel, Februar 1922. Einige Kinder spielen die Vermählung Prinzessin Marias, der Tochter König Georgs V., mit dem Grafen von Harewood nach. Dies war die erste königliche Hochzeit, die übertragen wurde, und sie wurde zu einem beliebten Kinderspiel.

Mariés pour de faux, février 1922. Des enfants jouent au mariage de la princesse Mary, fille du roi George V, et du comte de Harewood. Ce fut le premier mariage royal transmis en direct et il inspira un jeu que les enfants adoraient jouer.

3. Work
Arbeit
Le travail

A tough job, but lucky to get it. Construction workers installing tramlines, June 1929. The Wall Street Crash was only four months away, and that would create millions more unemployed.

Harte Arbeit, aber besser als keine. Bauarbeiter verlegen Straßenbahnschienen, Juni 1929. Bis zum „Schwarzen Freitag“ der New Yorker Börse waren es nur noch vier Monate, und Millionen Arbeitslose würden auf der Straße stehen.

Dur travail, mais c’est mieux que rien. Des ouvriers installent les voies d’un tram, juin 1929. Le krach de Wall Street aurait lieu quatre mois plus tard et allait créer des millions de chômeurs supplémentaires.

3. Work
Arbeit
Le travail

'When I finished my time after six and a half years as an apprentice shipwright, I had five days' work and then six and a half years on the dole' – Billy Rounce, British shipyard worker.

It was all too common a story. As in the Thirties, the spectre of unemployment brooded over the Twenties. In the hope that they would keep their jobs, both white-collar workers and blue-collar workers in London, Pittsburgh, Berlin, Marseille and a thousand other cities, accepted longer hours and less pay.

Not that the spirit of the workers was entirely broken. There were plenty of strikes in the Twenties. A million coal miners went on strike in Britain in 1920 and again in 1921. There were major rail strikes in the United States in 1920 and 1922, and in France in 1920, when one employer likened the proceedings to a civilian 'Battle of the Marne'.

The biggest strike of all was in Britain, in 1926, though it started as a lockout. Unions responded with a call for a general strike and, for a few days, the workers responded gallantly enough. But bit by bit they drifted back to work, until only the miners were left, bristling with fury, but sick at heart.

„Als ich nach sechseinhalb Jahren meine Ausbildung als Schiffsbauer abschloß, hatte ich fünf Tage lang Arbeit und war dann sechseinhalb Jahre arbeitslos", so Billy Rounce, ein britischer Werftarbeiter.

Dergleichen geschah leider sehr häufig. Wie ein Jahrzehnt später waren bereits in den zwanziger Jahren die Menschen von Arbeitslosigkeit bedroht. In der Hoffnung, daß sie ihre Arbeitsplätze behalten würden, nahmen in London, Pittsburgh, Berlin, Marseille und tausend anderen Städten Büroangestellte und Arbeiter längere Arbeitszeiten und eine schlechtere Bezahlung in Kauf.

Der Geist der Arbeiterschaft war jedoch nicht vollends gebrochen. So gab es auch in den zwanziger Jahren Streiks. Im Jahre 1920 und wiederum 1921 streikten eine Million Grubenarbeiter. 1920 und 1922 gab es in den Vereinigten Staaten große Eisenbahnerstreiks und ebenso in Frankreich 1920, wo ein Arbeitgeber die Vorgehensweise mit einer „Schlacht um die Marne" unter Zivilisten verglich.

Der größte Streik fand jedoch 1926 in Großbritannien statt. Er hatte ursprünglich als Aussperrung begonnen, auf die die Gewerkschaften mit einem Aufruf zum Generalstreik reagierten. Einige Tage lang folgten die Arbeiter tapfer diesem Aufruf. Doch nach und nach nahmen sie ihre Arbeit wieder auf, bis schließlich nur noch die Bergleute übrigblieben und ihrer Wut und ihrem Kummer Ausdruck verliehen.

« J'ai été apprenti charpentier pendant six ans et demi, ensuite j'ai travaillé cinq jours et après j'ai été au chômage pendant six ans et demi », Billy Rounce, charpentier d'un chantier naval britannique.

Cette histoire était celle de bien d'autres. Comme dans les années trente, le spectre du chômage pesa sur les années vingt. Que ce soit à Londres, à Pittsburgh, à Berlin, à Marseille ou dans n'importe quelle autre ville, les employés de bureau et les ouvriers acceptaient de faire des heures supplémentaires et d'être payés moins, dans l'espoir de conserver leur emploi.

La revendication syndicale ne fut pas étouffée pour autant et il y eut de nombreuses grèves. Un million de mineurs firent grève en Angleterre en 1920 puis en 1921. Il y eut de grandes grèves de cheminots aux Etats-Unis en 1920 et en 1922, ainsi qu'en France en 1920, où un patron compara l'événement à une « bataille civile de la Marne ».

Enfin, la grève la plus importante fut celle de 1926 en Grande-Bretagne, qui commença par la fermeture patronale d'usines. Les syndicats répondirent par un appel à la grève générale et, durant quelques jours, le monde ouvrier fit preuve de solidarité. Mais, peu à peu, tout le monde reprit le chemin du travail, laissant les mineurs défendre seuls leur cause, animés de colère et la mort dans l'âme.

An early car assembly line, 1920. 'People can have it any colour, so long as it's black' – Henry Ford. By the early Twenties, the Ford Motor Company was turning out over 4,000 cars a day.

Eines der ersten Montagebänder für Autos, 1920. „Unsere Kunden können die Wagen in jeder beliebigen Farbe bekommen, solange es Schwarz ist", erklärte einst Henry Ford. In den frühen zwanziger Jahren produzierte die Ford Motor Company bereits über 4.000 Autos pro Tag.

L'une des premières chaînes de montage de voitures, 1920. « Les gens peuvent choisir n'importe quelle couleur, du moment que c'est noir », Henry Ford. Au début des années vingt, les usines de la Ford Motor Company fabriquaient 4 000 voitures par jour.

Stacks of motor body parts at the Opel works in the late Twenties. The von Opel family were among the giants of the motor car industry. Fritz von Opel, son of the founder drove the first rocket-powered car. It accelerated from 0 to 100 kph (0 to 62 mph) in 8 seconds.

Gestapelte Karosserieteile in einer Fabrikhalle der Opel-Werke in den späten zwanziger Jahren. Die Familie von Opel gehörte zu den führenden Größen der Automobilindustrie. Fritz von Opel, der Sohn des Firmengründers, fuhr den ersten Wagen mit Raketenantrieb, der in 8 Sekunden von 0 auf 100 km/h beschleunigen konnte.

Piles de carrosseries dans les ateliers Opel à la fin des années vingt. La famille von Opel faisait partie des géants de l'industrie automobile. Fritz von Opel, le fils du fondateur, conduisit la première voiture à fusées. Elle pouvait atteindre la vitesse de 100 km/heure en 8 secondes.

Workers in uniforms and headscarves sort dried figs in a factory in Smyrna (Izmir), Turkey, 1925.

Arbeiterinnen in Arbeitskleidung und Kopftuch sortieren getrocknete Feigen in einer Fabrik in Smyrna (Izmir), Türkei, 1925.

Des ouvrières en uniforme et voilées trient des figues séchées dans une usine de Smyrne (Izmir), Turquie, 1925.

Coating biscuits with sugar in the W & R Jacob's factory, Liverpool, 1926. Even in poorer homes, there was great pressure on women to give up their jobs once they got married. A woman's place was still at the kitchen sink, rather than the factory bench.

In der Fabrik W. & R. Jacob in Liverpool werden Kekse mit einer Zuckerschicht überzogen, 1926. Selbst in den sozial schwächeren Kreisen erwartete man, daß Frauen nach der Hochzeit ihre Arbeit aufgaben. Der allgemeinen Vorstellung zufolge gehörte eine Ehefrau noch immer in die Küche und nicht in die Fabrik.

Glaçage de gâteaux à la fabrique W. & R. Jacob, Liverpool, 1926. Même chez les familles les plus modestes, les femmes étaient vivement encouragées à abandonner leur travail une fois mariées. La place de la femme était encore à la cuisine plutôt qu'à l'usine.

'All at once I saw a crowd, a host of golden daffodils… ten thousand saw I at a glance…' wrote William Wordsworth. But when you had to pack them, every day for as long as the season lasted, they didn't make you want to dance. Workers at Long Rock, Cornwall, 1926.

„Plötzlich sah ich eine Menge, ein ganzes Meer gold'ner Narzissen … Zehntausend sah ich auf einen Blick …", schrieb William Wordsworth. Doch wenn man sie verpacken mußte, tagaus, tagein, die ganze Saison hindurch, dann verspürte man bei ihrem Anblick wohl nicht mehr den Wunsch zu tanzen. Arbeiterinnen in Long Rock, Cornwall, 1926.

« Et soudain je vis un parterre de jonquilles… mon regard embrassait des milliers de jonquilles… », William Wordsworth. Mais, quand il s'agissait d'en faire des bouquets, chaque jour, aussi longtemps que durait la saison, l'enthousiasme n'était plus le même. Ouvrières à Long Rock, Cornouailles, 1926.

September 1927. Women agricultural workers bring in the maize harvest, Hoddesdon, Hertfordshire. Thousands of women had worked on the land during World War I.

September 1927. Landarbeiterinnen bei der Maisernte in Hoddesdon, Hertfordshire. Während des Ersten Weltkrieges hatten Tausende von Frauen in der Landwirtschaft gearbeitet.

Septembre 1927. Des ouvrières agricoles font la récolte du maïs, Hoddesdon, Hertfordshire. Des milliers de femmes avaient travaillé aux champs durant la Première Guerre mondiale.

A long hard pull to the top. Workmen climb a rope to scale one of the pillars of the Albert Bridge, London, October 1926.

Der Weg nach oben kostet einige Anstrengung. Arbeiter klettern an einem Seil empor, um von einem der Pfeiler der Albert Bridge abgeblätterte Farbe und Rost zu entfernen, London, Oktober 1926.

Longue ascension vers le sommet. Des ouvriers escaladent à la corde l'un des piliers du pont Albert à Londres, afin de la dérouiller, octobre 1926.

Mending the glass roof of the Crystal Palace in South London, June 1927. In all, the Palace was made up of two million square feet (189,000 square metres) of glass, so there was always enough work for the squad in this photograph.

Einige Handwerker bessern das Glasdach des Crystal Palace in Süd-London aus, Juni 1927. Da der Palast aus insgesamt 189.000 Quadratmetern Glas bestand, brauchten sich diese Herren um ausreichende Arbeit nicht zu sorgen.

Soudure sur la verrière du Crystal Palace, Sud-Londres, juin 1927. Le palais comptait une surface en verre de 189 000 mètres carrés. Aussi l'équipe de soudeurs, à l'œuvre sur ce cliché, ne manquait-elle jamais de travail.

April 1926. Four men walk along the top of the Brooklyn Bridge, New York City. It was part of a test for those who wished to be employed to paint the bridge.

April 1926. Vier Arbeiter überqueren in schwindelerregender Höhe die New Yorker Brooklyn Bridge. Dieser Gang gehörte zum Auswahlverfahren der Arbeiter, die sich zum Streichen der Brücke gemeldet hatten.

Avril 1926. Quatre hommes marchent le long d'une rampe sur le pont de Brooklyn à New York. Cet exercice était un test pour ceux qui désiraient être engagés pour peindre le pont.

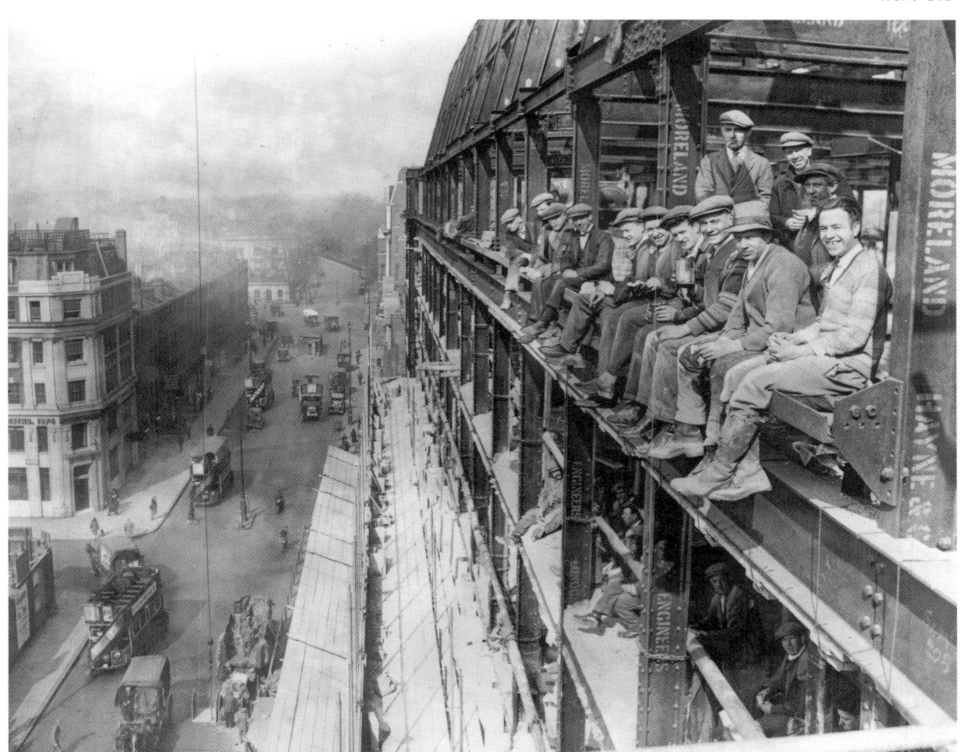

April 1929. Construction workers take a lunch break high above the streets of London. Today, it would be impossible to find any street in London with so little traffic at midday.

April 1929. Bauarbeiter genießen ihre Mittagspause hoch über den Straßen Londons. Heutzutage wäre es unmöglich, in der britischen Metropole eine Straße zu finden, in der um die Mittagszeit so wenig Verkehr herrscht.

Avril 1929. Des ouvriers font une pause à l'heure du déjeuner, très haut perchés au dessus des rues de Londres. Aujourd'hui, il serait difficile de trouver une rue de Londres avec aussi peu de circulation à cette heure-ci de la journée.

Building the tunnels for the new Piccadilly Underground Station, February 1927. It was a spectacular challenge. The decision to rebuild meant removing the statue of Eros and digging out a labyrinth of tunnels, installing lifts, escalators and an Art Deco shopping arcade.

Bau eines Tunnels für die neue U-Bahn-Station am Piccadilly Circus, Februar 1927. Es war eine unglaubliche Herausforderung. Für den Bau mußte die Eros-Statue vom Platz entfernt werden, und es entstand ein Labyrinth von Tunnelgängen, Aufzugschächten, Rolltreppen und eine Einkaufspassage im Art-Déco-Stil.

Construction de la nouvelle station de métro à Piccadilly, février 1927. Ce chantier était un défi incroyable, nécessitant le déplacement de la statue d'Eros, la percée de nombreux tunnels, l'installation d'ascenseurs et d'escaliers roulants et l'aménagement d'une galerie marchande Art Déco.

The salt mines, British style, Cheshire, 1929. Unlike their opposite numbers in the Soviet Union, workers here had not been exiled, but the job was still back-breaking.

Ein Salzbergwerk im britischen Stil, Cheshire, 1929. Die Arbeiter befanden sich hier zwar nicht in der Verbannung wie ihre Kollegen in der Sowjetunion, doch ihre Arbeit war ebenso anstrengend.

Mines de sel, façon britannique, Cheshire, 1929. Au contraire de leurs collègues soviétiques, les ouvriers de cette mine n'avaient pas été exilés de force. Leur travail n'en était pas moins pénible.

Coils of steel. Making bed springs in a British factory, 1925.

Aufgerollter Stahl. In einer britischen Fabrik werden Sprungfedern für Betten hergestellt, 1925.

Fils de fer. Fabrication de ressorts de lits dans une usine britannique, 1925.

Coils of pasta. Men operating a macaroni machine in Naples, January 1929.

Aufgerollte Pasta. Zwei Arbeiter bedienen eine Makkaroni-Maschine in Neapel, Januar 1929.

Fils de pâtes. Des ouvriers travaillant sur une machine à fabriquer des macaronis à Naples, janvier 1929.

Busy line. Women stamping out the dial pieces for new automatic telephones in a factory in Britain, November 1924. The telephone had ceased to be merely the toy of the rich, and was by then installed in millions of homes and offices.

Britische Arbeiterinnen stanzen Wählscheiben für neue automatische Telefonapparate, November 1924. Das Telefon war zu dieser Zeit nicht länger ein Spielzeug der Reichen. Es hielt nicht zur Einzug in die Geschäftswelt, sondern auch in Millionen von Privathaushalten.

Ouvrières sur une chaîne de montage d'une usine fabriquant les nouveaux téléphones automatiques, Grande-Bretagne, novembre 1924. Le téléphone n'était plus un jouet réservé aux riches, mais un appareil désormais installé dans des millions de foyers et de bureaux.

A rare sight on the streets – a black woman taxi driver in Paris, 1929.

Ein seltener Anblick – eine schwarze Taxifahrerin in Paris, 1929.

Fait rare – une femme noire, chauffeur de taxi à Paris, 1929.

Nurses at the Foundling Hospital, London, put up Christmas decorations, 1925. The following year, the hospital moved to Redhill in Surrey.

Schwestern im Londoner Findelheim schmücken den Speisesaal für die Weihnachtsfeier, 1925. Ein Jahr später wurde das Heim nach Redhill in die Grafschaft Surrey verlegt.

Des infirmières de l'orphelinat à Londres suspendent les décorations de Noël, 1925. L'orphelinat déménagea l'année suivante à Redhill dans le Surrey, Angleterre.

Cleaners give a polish to the LNER locomotive *Pretty Polly*, January 1928. The railways were still massive employers of labour.

Reinigungspersonal bringt die LNER-Lokomotive *Pretty Polly* auf Hochglanz, Januar 1928. Die Eisenbahngesell-schaften waren wichtige Arbeitgeber.

Nettoyage de la locomotive LNER, *Pretty Polly*, janvier 1928. Les compagnies des chemins de fer embauchaient alors en masse.

Playing with the real thing – volunteer workers maintain part of the track during the General Strike in 1926. Of all the blackleg occupations, working on the railways was the most popular.

Eisenbahnspiel für Erwachsene – Freiwillige helfen während des Generalstreiks von 1926 bei der Streckenwartung. Die Arbeit bei der Eisenbahn war die beliebteste der möglichen Beschäftigungen, um den Streik zu brechen.

Jouer pour de vrai – des volontaires au travail pour permettre la circulation de quelques trains pendant la grève générale de 1926. Parmi toutes les activités proposées pour briser la grève, celle-ci était la plus populaire.

Home from home. An office worker, probably a manager, prepares for sleep in his temporary bed during the British transport strike of 1924.

Weit weg von zu Hause und dennoch daheim. Ein leitender Angestellter bereitet sich während des britischen Transportstreiks von 1924 auf eine Nacht im Büro vor.

A la maison loin de chez soi. Un employé de bureau, probablement chef de service, se prépare à dormir dans un lit de fortune durant la grève des transports de 1924 en Grande-Bretagne.

A commuter roller-skates to work during the General Strike, May 1926. He has determination, his lunch, and a cold. The white sweater with its club bands betrays his class origins.

Ein Pendler fährt während des Generalstreiks auf Rollschuhen ins Büro, Mai 1926. Er besitzt Entschlossenheit, ein Sandwich und eine Erkältung. Die Clubstreifen seines hellen Pullovers weisen auf seine soziale Klasse hin.

Un banlieusard va travailler en patins à roulettes pendant la grève générale, mai 1926. Il semble déterminé, prenant son déjeuner et un bon rhume. Le pull blanc à rayures trahit ses origines sociales.

Oxford University student volunteers parade as special police constables, May 1926. Few young people from working-class homes would have found their way to university in the Twenties, so these gallant 'toffs' are looking forward to a class war.

Studenten der Universität Oxford melden sich als freiwillige Hilfspolizisten, Mai 1926. Da in den zwanziger Jahren nur wenige Jugendliche der Arbeiterschicht eine Universität besuchten, freuen sich die „feinen Herren" auf dieser Aufnahme auf den bevorstehenden Klassenkampf.

Des étudiants d'Oxford transformés en auxiliaires de police volontaires, mai 1926. Dans les années vingt, rares étaient les enfants d'ouvriers qui parvenaient jusqu'à l'université. Quant à ces élégants « aristos », ils semblent prêts pour la lutte des classes.

An official of the Trade Workers' Union hands out strike pay, Camberwell, March 1924. This weekly allowance was £1 for each man, plus two shillings (10p) for each of his children.

Ein Funktionär der Arbeitergewerkschaft zahlt in Camberwell Streikgelder aus, März 1924. Die finanzielle Unterstützung betrug pro Woche 1 Pfund für jeden Arbeiter und 2 Shilling (10 Pence) für jedes seiner Kinder.

Un responsable du Syndicat des Travailleurs donne à chaque gréviste son « salaire de grève », Camberwell, mars 1924. L'indemnité pour la semaine s'élevait à 1 £ par homme plus deux shillings (10 pence) par enfant.

May 1926. Special constables are issued with truncheons during the General Strike at Hornsey, London. By the time the strike ended, some 4,000 people had been arrested for violence, mainly in London, Glasgow, and the mining districts.

Mai 1926. Im Londoner Stadtteil Hornsey werden Hilfspolizisten mit Gummiknüppeln ausgerüstet. Bis zum Ende des Generalstreiks wurden vor allem in London, Glasgow und in den Bergbaugebieten etwa 4.000 Menschen wegen Gewalttätigkeiten festgenommen.

Mai 1926. Distribution de matraques aux auxiliaires de police durant la grève générale, Hornsey, Londres. A la fin de la grève, 4 000 personnes avaient été arrêtées pour actes de violence, surtout à Londres, Glasgow et dans les régions minières.

The joys of point duty. A Birmingham policeman (above) stands on a rubber mat while directing traffic. A Yorkshire policeman (right) stands on a pile of straw to keep his feet warm. Both these pictures were taken in 1926, a busy year for the police.

Die Freuden der Verkehrspolizei. Ein Polizist in Birmingham (oben) steht auf einer Gummimatte, während er den Verkehr regelt. Ein Polizist in Yorkshire (rechts) hat seine Füße mit Reisig bedeckt, um sie warmzuhalten. Beide Aufnahmen stammen aus dem Jahre 1926, einem Jahr, das die Polizei in Atem hielt.

Les joies de l'agent de la circulation. A Birmingham, un policier (ci-dessus) se tient debout sur un paillasson pendand qu'il dirige la circulation. Dans le Yorkshire, un policier (à droite) a recouvert ses pieds de paille pour ne pas avoir froid. Ces deux clichés datent de 1926, une année très mouvementée pour la police.

L N E R
COODS AND COAL DEPOT
RUDOLPH
VALENTINO
A SAINTED DEVIL

Happier days for the boys in blue. Police hold back the crowds during the wedding of the Earl of Harewood to Princess Mary at Saint Margaret's Westminster, July 1922. This was the wedding that inspired a children's game (see p.89).

Angenehmere Tage für die Polizei. Jubelnde Menschenmengen feiern vor der Kirche St. Margaret's in Westminster die Eheschließung des Grafen von Harewood mit Prinzessin Maria, Juli 1922. Es war jene Hochzeit, die Kinder gerne nachstellten (siehe S. 89).

Jours de fête pour les agents de police, censés contenir la foule lors du mariage du duc de Harewood à la princesse Mary à l'église Sainte-Margaret de Westminster, juillet 1922. C'est ce mariage qui inspira aux enfants un jeu (voir p. 89).

Two aspects of police work. A London copper escorts a group of charming children across an empty street in Chelsea, September 1928.

Zwei Aspekte der Polizeiarbeit. Ein Londoner Polizist geleitet eine Gruppe netter Kinder über eine leere Straße im Stadtteil Chelsea, September 1928.

Deux aspects du travail de la police. Un policier de Londres aide un groupe d'adorables enfants à traverser une rue déserte de Chelsea, septembre 1928.

A London policewoman chases a gang of naked youths from the Serpentine, Hyde Park, 1926. This is the retribution that followed the happy dive into the water shown on pages 144–5.

Eine Londoner Polizistin jagt eine Schar nackter Jungen die im Serpentine-See im Hyde Park gebadet hatten, 1926. Dies war die Folge des unbekümmerten Sprungs ins kühle Naß auf der Seite 144–5.

Une femme agent de police chasse une bande de garçons qui nageaient nus dans le lac Serpentine, Hyde Park, 1926. C'est la réprimande annoncée après le joyeux plongeon dans le lac montré aux pages 144–5.

Bold Gendarme. A French policeman takes aim while on a weapons-training course in Paris, 1929. There was little unrest in Paris that year, but perhaps he fancied taking a potshot at the odd Surrealist.

Ein kühner Gendarme. Ein Pariser Polizist bei einem Waffenausbildungskurs, 1929. In jenem Jahr gab es in der Stadt kaum Unruhen, doch vielleicht verspürte er Lust, den einen oder anderen Surrealisten aufs Korn zu nehmen.

Gendarme frondeur. Un policier français vise sa cible durant une séance d'entraînement à Paris, 1929. Paris n'avait pas connu beaucoup d'agitations cette année-là, mais peut-être l'homme avait-il envie de mettre en joue quelque surréaliste intempestif.

A police pistol-shooting competition at Petersham, near London, 1922. There have always been many exceptions to the general belief that the British police are unarmed.

Ein Polizeiwettbewerb im Pistolenschießen in Petersham bei London, 1922. Es gab immer wieder Ausnahmen, daß britische Polizisten – gemäß der allgemeinen Überzeugung – unbewaffnet seien.

Tournoi de tir de la police à Petersham, près de Londres, 1922. Nombreuses sont les exceptions contredisant l'idée reçue selon laquelle la police britannique n'est pas armée.

The main vault of the strong room at the Cleveland Trust Company, Ohio, USA, 1924, in the early days of Al Capone and 'Bugs' Moran.

Der Haupttresorraum der Stahlkammer der Cleveland Trust Company in Ohio, USA, 1924. Damals begannen die großen Zeiten der Gangsterbosse Al Capone und „Bugs“ Moran.

La voûte principale de la chambre forte de la Cleveland Trust Company, Ohio, Etats-Unis, 1924, au debut de l'époque d'Al Capone et de « Bugs » Moran.

A training exercise for a member of the German army, Berlin, 1925. It is impossible to discern whether the victim represents a communist, a fascist, a saboteur or a spy, but both men seem to be taking the exercise very seriously.

Eine Ausbildungsübung für einen Soldaten der deutschen Reichswehr, Berlin, 1925. Es ist nicht zu erkennen, ob das Opfer einen Kommunisten, einen Faschisten, einen Saboteur oder einen Spion darstellen soll, aber beide Herren scheinen die Übung überaus ernst zu nehmen.

Séance d'entraînement pour un soldat allemand, Berlin, 1925. Il est impossible de deviner si la victime incarne un communiste, un fasciste, un saboteur ou un espion. Reste que les deux hommes semblent prendre leur exercice très au sérieux.

A member of the Achille Serre Ladies' Fire Brigade in London, April 1926. Achille Serre ran a chain of dry-cleaning shops.

Eine Feuerwehrfrau von Achille Serres Ladies' Fire Brigade in London, April 1926. Achille Serre betrieb eine Kette von chemischen Reinigungen.

L'une des femmes pompiers de la brigade féminine d'Achille Serre, Londres, avril 1926. Achille Serre possédait une chaîne de blanchisseries.

April 1924.
Mary P Allen, Commandant of the Women's Auxiliary Police Force arrives in New York from London. She wished to study American police methods.

April 1924.
Die Kommandantin der Londoner Frauenabteilung der Hilfspolizei, Mary P. Allen, bei ihrer Ankunft in New York. Sie wollte sich mit den amerikanischen Polizeimethoden vertraut zu machen.

Avril 1924.
Arrivée à New York de Mary P. Allen, commandant de la police auxiliaire féminine de Londres. Elle souhaitait étudier les méthodes de la police américaine.

Members of the London Fire Brigade tackle a blaze at Chapman's Wharf, Shad Thames, August 1928. They are standing on a fire float, a special boat with machinery on board to pump water from the Thames.

Londoner Feuerwehrmänner bekämpfen einen Brand in Chapman's Wharf, Shad Thames, August 1928. Sie befinden sich auf einem Feuerlöschboot, dessen spezielle Pumpausrüstung das Wasser der Themse für den Einsatz nutzbar macht.

Des pompiers londoniens tentent de maîtriser un incendie sur le quai Chapman à Shad Thames, août 1928. Ils œuvrent à partir d'une embarcation spéciale équipée d'une pompe à eau alimentée par la Tamise.

Avoiding meltdown. A fireman struggles from Madame Tussaud's, carrying one of the waxworks saved from the flames when the museum caught fire, March 1925.

Ein Feuerwehrmann versucht beim Brand von Madame Tussaud's Wachsfigurenkabinett Figuren vor den Flammen zu retten, März 1925.

Empêcher que la cire ne fonde. Un pompier aux prises avec l'une des statues de cire du musée Tussaud, sauvée des flammes lors de l'incendie qui ravagea le musée, mars 1925.

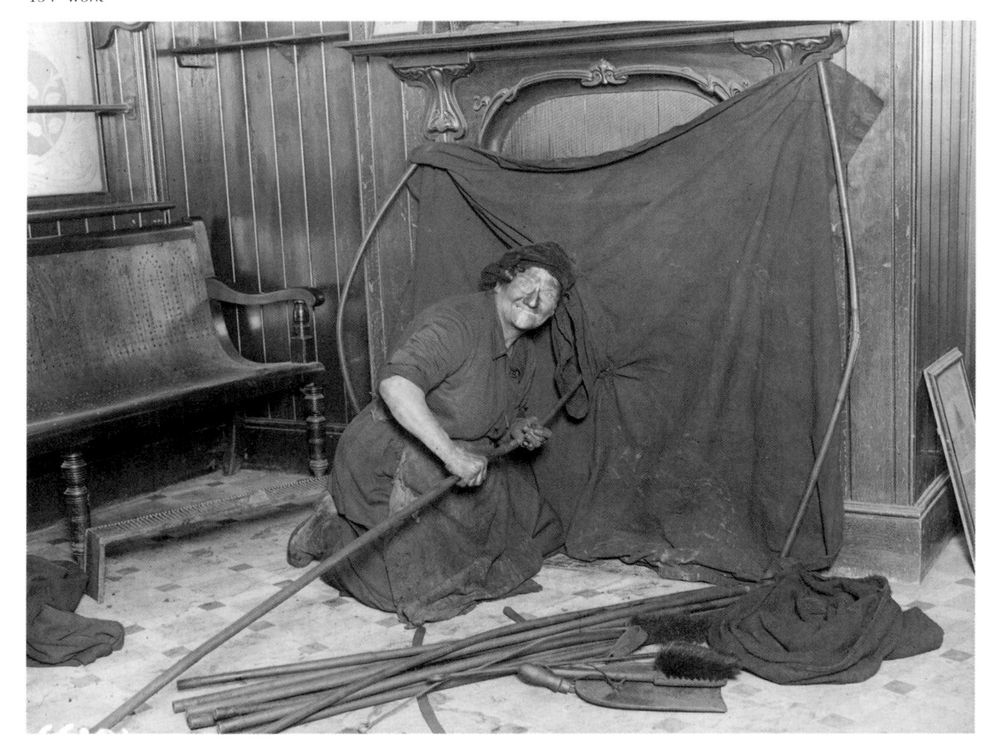

A clean sweep. Mrs Nelsong of Clapton, East London, at work, 1928. Mrs Nelsong was one of the very few women chimney-sweeps at that or any other time.

Saubere Arbeit. Mrs. Nelsong aus dem Ost-Londoner Stadtteil Clapton bei der Arbeit, 1928. Weibliche Schornsteinfeger waren damals wie heute sehr selten.

Souci de propreté. Mme Nelsong de Clapton, est de Londres, au travail, 1928. L'une des rares femmes ramoneurs que la profession ait jamais comptée, que ce soit à cette époque ou à une autre.

Hard as nails. Annie Clubb, the only woman practising as a blacksmith in London, and possibly in England, 1928. She had been in the business for 25 years, and specialized in making iron balconies, window frames, and decorative panels.

Hart wie Stahl. Annie Clubb war die einzige Frau Londons und wahrscheinlich ganz Englands, die als Schmied ihr Geld verdiente, 1928. Zu diesem Zeitpunkt war sie bereits seit 25 Jahren im Geschäft und spezialisiert auf die Herstellung von schmiedeeisernen Balkonen, Fensterrahmen und dekorativen Platten.

Dur comme fer. Annie Clubb, la seule femme forgeron de Londres et peut-être d'Angleterre, 1928. Dans le métier depuis 25 ans, elle s'était spécialisée dans les balustrades de balcons, les cadres de fenêtre en fer forgé et les plaques décoratives.

A group of ex-servicemen set off for work, 1920. Two years before they had risked their lives in the trenches, now they spent their days hawking on the streets. Very soon they would become 'forgotten men'.

Ehemalige Soldaten auf dem Weg zur Arbeit, 1920. Zwei Jahre zuvor hatten sie noch ihr Leben im Schützengraben riskiert. Nun verdienten sie ihr Geld als Straßenverkäufer. Schon sehr bald sollten sie zu „vergessenen Männern" werden.

Des anciens combattants prêts à travailler, 1920. Deux ans plus tôt, ils avaient risqué leur vie dans les tranchées; là, ils passaient leurs journées dans la rue à vendre à la criée et bientôt ils ne seraient plus que des « hommes oubliés ».

A toy seller on the steps of St Martin-in-the-Fields, London, 1928.

Ein Spielzeugverkäufer auf der Treppe der Londoner Kirche St. Martin-in-the-Fields, 1928.

Un vendeur de jouets en peluche sur les marches de l'église de St. Martin-in-the-Fields à Londres, 1928.

The Imperfectly Packed Parcel department at a post office, 1926. 'Imperfectly Packed' seems a mild way to describe the piles of ill-wrapped, disintegrating packages that litter the counter.

In der Abteilung für mangelhaft verpackte Pakete eines Postamtes, 1926. „Mangelhaft verpackt“ scheint ein milder Ausdruck zu sein für den Stapel schlecht verschnürter Bündel, mit denen dieser Schalter übersät ist.

Bureau des paquets mal emballés dans une poste, 1926. « Mal emballés » est un doux euphémisme pour décrire cette pile de paquets ne tenant plus que par des bouts de ficelles et qui encombrent ce comptoir.

IMPERFECTLY
PACKED
PARCELS

4. Leisure
Freizeit
Les loisirs

British comedian George Graves and his wife, the actress Flora Courtenay, slide down the 'Jack and Jill' helter-skelter in the amusement park of the British Empire Exhibition, Wembley, London 1924. Twenty seven million people visited the exhibition.

Der britische Komiker George Graves und seine Ehefrau, die Schauspielerin Flora Courtenay, auf der Riesenrutschbahn im Vergnügungspark der Londoner Ausstellung des Britischen Weltreichs in Wembley, 1924. Siebenundzwanzig Millionen Menschen besuchten diese Ausstellung.

L'humoriste britannique George Graves et sa femme, la comédienne Flora Courtenay, sur le toboggan géant au parc d'attractions de l'Exposition de l'Empire britannique, Wembley, Londres, 1924. Vingt-sept millions de personnes visitèrent l'exposition.

4. Leisure
Freizeit
Les loisirs

Until the fun-loving Twenties came along, the concept of recreation was almost unknown. People took days off, and went for cycle rides, the well-to-do managed a week or two by the seaside – but the notion that you could regularly find time to play was one of the happier innovations of the Jazz Age.

It was instantaneously attractive. Cheap tickets were available to visit the country or the seaside, and even in the big cities there were parks and fairgrounds and recreation grounds. Conscious that a happy and healthy population is less likely to cause trouble than a discontented, ailing one, governments encouraged people to take to the great outdoors.

Amateur sport became more and more popular. In suburbs all over the Western world, tennis clubs, golf clubs and football clubs sprang up. People learnt to ride horses, to shoot with bow and arrow, to swim, to fish, to sail. And if such activity was too expensive or too exhausting, they simply paddled in the sea or walked in the countryside.

It was as though a new-found freedom had possessed them. Life didn't have to be unmitigated toil and drudgery – there was such a thing as the weekend, the bank holiday, the day out, the great escape…

Bis die vergnügungssüchtigen zwanziger Jahre Einzug hielten, war Freizeit so gut wie unbekannt. Man nahm sich ab und zu einen Tag frei und machte eine Radtour. Die Wohlhabenderen leisteten sich sogar ein bis zwei Wochen am Meer – doch die Vorstellung, daß man sich regelmäßig Zeit zum Entspannen gönnen konnte, war eine der positiven Neuerungen des Jazz-Zeitalters.

Das Freizeit-Konzept hatte einen durchschlagenden Erfolg. Es gab Fahrkarten zu Sondertarifen für Reisen aufs Land oder ans Meer, und selbst in den Großstädten wurden

Parks, Rummelplätze und Spielplätze angelegt. In dem Bewußtsein, daß eine glückliche und gesunde Bevölkerung weniger Unruhe stiftet als eine unzufriedene und kränkelnde, ermunterten die Regierungen das Volk, sich in die freie Natur zu begeben.

Der Amateursport wurde immer beliebter. Überall in der westlichen Hemisphäre gründete man in den Vororten Tennis- und Golfclubs und Fußballvereine. Man lernte Reiten, Bogenschießen, Schwimmen, Angeln und Segeln. Und wem solcherlei Aktivitäten zu kostspielig oder zu anstrengend waren, der schlenderte einfach den Strand entlang oder unternahm lange Spaziergänge.

Es schien, als habe eine neue Freiheit von den Menschen Besitz ergriffen. Das Leben mußte offenbar nicht nur aus Mühen und stumpfsinniger Plackerei bestehen. Es gab das Wochenende, Feiertage und Ausflüge, die große Flucht…

Avant l'arrivée des années vingt une décennie dédiée à l'amusement le concept de divertissement était pratiquement inconnu. Les gens qui avaient quelques jours de congé partaient faire des excursions à vélo tandis que les plus nantis s'offraient une semaine ou deux au bord de la mer – mais l'idée de prendre régulièrement le temps de s'amuser fut une des innovations les plus heureuses de l'age du jazz.

Soudain, tout fut accessible. Il était possible d'aller à la campagne ou au bord de la mer pour un prix raisonnable, tandis que les grandes villes érigeaient des parcs d'attractions, des foires et des lieux de récréation. Conscients qu'un peuple heureux et en bonne santé serait moins enclin à contester qu'un peuple mécontent et malade, les gouvernements faisaient tout pour encourager les gens à profiter des distractions en plein air.

Le sport amateur était de plus en plus populaire. Aux portes des villes occidentales, on construisait des clubs de tennis, de golf et de football. Les gens se mirent à pratiquer l'équitation, le tir à l'arc, la natation, la pêche et la voile. Et si ces activités étaient trop chères ou trop fatigantes, ils pataugeaient tout simplement au bord de la mer ou se promenaient à la campagne.

C'était comme si le monde avait découvert une nouvelle forme de liberté. La vie n'était pas seulement faite de travail et de corvées, il y avait aussi le week-end, les jours fériés, les sorties, la grande évasion…

A group of naked boys leap into the Serpentine at Hyde Park, London, during the heat wave of 1926. Although the need to cool down could not be denied, retribution was to come (see p. 125).

Eine Gruppe nackter Jungen springt während der Hitzewelle von 1926 in den Serpentine-See im Londoner Hyde Park. Obwohl die Notwendigkeit, sich abzukühlen, nicht von der Hand zu weisen war, sollte diese Aktion nicht ohne Folgen bleiben (siehe S. 125).

Un groupe de garçons nus saute dans le lac Serpentine à Hyde Park, Londres, durant la vague de chaleur de 1926. Le besoin de fraîcheur est indéniable, mais la réprimande n'allait pas tarder (voir p. 125).

February 1925. Members of the Brighton Swimming Club tone up with some exercises on the beach. The date indicates that these were no mere fair-weather swimmers – they were hardy souls who braved the sea at all times of year.

Februar 1925. Mitglieder des Schwimmvereins von Brighton wärmen sich mit ein paar Turnübungen am Strand auf. Das Datum verrät es, daß diese abgehärteten Schwimmer der See zu jeder Jahreszeit trotzten.

Février 1925. Des membres du club de natation de Brighton s'échauffent sur la plage. La date indique qu'il ne s'agit pas de nageurs occasionnels, mais de sportifs endurcis nageant par n'importe quel temps tout au long de l'année.

Fun on the sand at Shanklin, Isle of Wight, 1928. Then, as always, the seaside brought out the primitive best, and beast, in people.

Strandspaß in Shanklin auf der Isle of Wight, 1928. Schon damals brachte der Urlaub am Meer nicht nur das Beste, sondern auch das Biest im Menschen zum Vorschein.

Jeux de plage à Shanklin, île de Wight, 1928. A la mer, les gens inventaient toutes sortes de jeux qui pouvaient être aussi drôles que primitifs.

Ice maidens play cards, August 1929. Although they had been banned earlier even in such holiday havens as Atlantic City, by the late Twenties the one-piece bathing costume was perfectly acceptable to all but the most prudish.

Eisgekühlte junge Damen beim Kartenspiel, August 1929. Obwohl der einteilige Badeanzug selbst in Ferienparadiesen wie Atlantic City zuvor verboten gewesen war, wurde er in den späten zwanziger Jahren bis auf wenige Ausnahmen von der Allgemeinheit akzeptiert.

Jeux de cartes sur glace, août 1929. Peu de temps auparavant, il était encore interdit de se mettre en maillot de bain une pièce, même dans un lieu de vacances aussi paradisiaque qu'Atlantic City mais, à la fin des années vingt, c'était devenu tout à fait courant, sauf pour les plus prudes.

1929. If you were excessively modest, you could always use the 'skreenette' to hide your embarrassment as you changed on the beach.

1929. Wer besonders schamhaft war, konnte eine „Skreenette" als Umkleidekabine verwenden, um Peinlichkeiten am Strand zu vermeiden.

1929. Si vous étiez très pudique, vous pouviez utiliser l'une de ces cabines portables, une « skreenette », pour vous changer sur la plage, à l'abri des regards indiscrets.

Brighton Pier, 1929. It could be the depths of winter, but it could as easily be a summer bank holiday on the south coast of England. The best thing to do was to head for a meal of fish and chips, and then home.

Der Pier von Brighton, 1929. So konnte an der Südküste Englands nicht nur ein stürmischer Wintertag aussehen, sondern auch ein Ferientag im Sommer. Bei solchem Wetter ging man am besten irgendwo Fish and Chips essen und fuhr anschließend wieder nach Hause.

Le quai de Brighton, 1929. Peut-être est-ce le plein hiver ou un jour de vacances en été, tout est possible sur la côte sud de l'Angleterre. La meilleure chose à faire est alors d'aller manger du poisson et des frites, puis de rentrer à la maison.

A group of workers from Tickler's Jam factory on an outing to Hastings on the south coast of England, September 1923. 'Beside the sea is where I'd like to be, there are lots of girls besides I should like to be beside, beside the seaside, beside the sea' – popular song.

Arbeiterinnen der Marmeladenfabrik Tickler auf einem Ausflug nach Hastings an der Südküste Englands, September 1923. „Am Meer, da möchte ich sein, denn dort sieht man viele Mädchen, außerdem möchte ich gerne am Meer sein, Meer sein, Meer sein ...," heißt es in einem britischen Volkslied.

Des ouvrières de l'usine de confiture Tickler en excursion à Hastings sur la côte sud de l'Angleterre, septembre 1923. « J'aimerais être au bord de la mer, où il y a plein de jolies filles, c'est là que j'aimerais être, à côté d'elles, au bord de l'eau, au bord de la mer » – chanson populaire.

June 1922. A family paddles together at Clacton, Essex. They are looking in the general direction of the Netherlands, though it is highly unlikely that any of them will ever go there – the days of package holidays abroad were generations away.

Juni 1922. Eine Familie nimmt im ein Fußbad am Strand von Clacton in Essex. Ihr Blick schweift in Richtung Holland, das wohl keiner von ihnen je besuchen wird – Pauschalreisen ins Ausland sollten erst Generationen später populär werden.

Juin 1922. Famille les pieds dans l'eau à Clacton, Essex. Ils regardent tous du côté des Pays-Bas, même s'il y a peu de chance qu'ils y aillent un jour – il faudra attendre encore plusieurs générations avant de pouvoir songer à des vacances organisées à l'étranger.

July 1929. Members of the Mermaids Swimming Club take the plunge at Highgate, London.

Juli 1929. Mitglieder des Meerjungfrauen-Schwimmvereins wagen diesen Sprung ins kühle Naß im Londoner Stadtviertel Highgate.

Juillet 1929. Des membres du club de natation des Sirènes se jettent à l'eau à Highgate, Londres.

Fay Webb and Louise Lorraine on the MGM lot, 1929. Louise Lorraine was 'exceptionally lovely' and the second "Jane" in Tarzan films. Fay Webb was the second wife of the singer and film star Rudy Vallee.

Fay Webb und Louise Lorraine auf dem MGM-Filmstudiogelände, 1929. Louise Lorraine galt als „ausgesprochen hübsch" und war die zweite Schauspielerin, die die Rolle der „Jane" in einem Tarzanfilm spielte. Fay Webb war die zweite Ehefrau des Sängers und Filmstars Rudy Vallee.

Fay Webb et Louise Lorraine dans l'enceinte des studios de la MGM, 1929. Louise Lorraine, « incroyablement ravissante », fut la deuxième « Jane » des films de Tarzan. Fay Webb était la deuxième femme du chanteur et célèbre acteur Rudy Vallee.

Anyone for pelota? The photograph was taken in England in 1925, though pelota was then almost exclusively a Basque game, played in France, Spain, and parts of the United States.

Wer spielt mit Pelota? Diese Aufnahme entstand 1925 in England, obwohl das baskische, tennisähnliche Rückschlagspiel damals fast ausschließlich in Frankreich, Spanien und Teilen der Vereinigten Staaten populär war.

Qui joue à la pelote basque ? Cette photographie, prise en Angleterre, date de 1925. A cette époque, ce jeu d'origine basque s'était déjà répandu en France, en Espagne et dans certaines régions des Etats-Unis.

April 1925. Another novelty night at the East Ham Palais de Danse, London. The dancers are struggling for the prizes hidden in the crackers – boxes of cigarettes.

April 1925. Eine weitere Nacht der Neuheiten im Palais de Danse in East Ham, London. Diesmal wetteifern die Tänzer um die in den Knallbonbons versteckten Gewinne – Zigarettenschachteln.

Avril 1925. Encore une soirée nouveauté au Palais de Danse d'East Ham, Londres. Les danseurs essaient d'attraper les prix – des paquets de cigarettes – cachés dans les diablotins.

February 1925. Members of the Brighton Swimming Club recover from their dip. It was reputedly a 'mild and sunny day', and what better after any brisk exercise than to fill your lungs with the mild taste of a good cigarette?

Februar 1925. Weibliche Mitglieder des Schwimmvereins von Brighton erholen sich vom Bad im kühlen Naß. Es soll ein „milder und sonniger Tag" gewesen sein, und was ist wohl nach einer regen sportlichen Betätigung schöner, als sich die Lungen mit einer guten Zigarette zu füllen?

Février 1925. Des membres du club de natation de Brighton récupèrent après la baignade. C'était une journée « douce et ensoleillée » et quoi de plus agréable, après avoir bien nagé, que d'aspirer une douce et délicieuse fumée de cigarette ?

December 1926. The Giant Lake fairy caves at Arding and Hobbs department store, Clapham, London. Every large store created a special grotto at Christmas time, where Santa was to be found, handing out presents to little children and wondering where his next employment would come from.

Dezember 1926. Diese Feengrotte im Riesen-See gehörte zur Weihnachtsdekoration des Kaufhauses Arding and Hobbs, Clapham, London. Jedes große Kaufhaus gestaltete zur Weihnachtszeit eine besondere Grotte, in der ein Weihnachtsmann Geschenke an kleine Kinder verteilte und sich unterdessen fragte, womit er wohl nach dem Fest sein Brot verdienen würde.

Décembre 1926. La grotte aux fées dans le lac géant du magasin Arding and Hobbs à Clapham, Londres. A Noël, tous les grands magasins avaient une grotte avec un Père Noël qui distribuait des cadeaux aux petits enfants, tout en se demandant quel serait son prochain travail.

April 1929. Professional motorcycle riders take time off from the dirt track to enjoy the thrills of a flying-boat ride in the Crystal Palace fairground, London. Until it was destroyed by fire in 1936, Crystal Palace was the Londoner's playground.

April 1929. Einige Motorradrennfahrer erholen sich vom Staub der Aschenbahn und genießen eine Flugboot-Runde im Londoner Vergnügungspark Crystal Palace. Bevor Crystal Palace 1936 bei einem Brand zerstört wurde, war dieses Gelände der Freizeitpark der Londoner.

Avril 1929. Des motocyclistes professionnels se divertissent loin des pistes poussiéreuses en faisant un tour en bateau volant à la foire du Crystal Palace, Londres. Ce parc d'attractions, si cher aux Londoniens, fut détruit par le feu en 1936.

The June race meeting at Brooklands, 1922. Advice to aspiring drivers on this circuit included, 'Smoking in a racing car is heavily frowned upon,' and 'Do not grouse at every difficulty; motor racing would be quite dull if there were no difficulties.'

Das Juni-Rennen in Brooklands, 1922. Zu den Ratschlägen, die den Fahrern ans Herz gelegt wurden, gehörte unter anderem: „Das Rauchen im Rennwagen wird stärkstens mißbilligt" und „Beklagen Sie sich nicht über jedes Problem; Autorennen wären sehr langweilig, wenn es keine Probleme gäbe".

Course de voitures à Brooklands, juin 1922. Parmi les conseils donnés aux concurrents, on pouvait lire « fumer dans une voiture de course est sévèrement désapprouvé » et « ne pas râler devant chaque obstacle ; la course serait ennuyeuse s'il n'y avait pas d'obstacles ».

Whitsun Bank Holiday 1924. The joys and terrors of the merry-go-round, British Empire Exhibition, Wembley, London. In the words of Patrick Chalmers, 'What's lost on the roundabouts we pull up on the swings.'

Pfingsten 1924. Die Freuden und Ängste des Karussellfahrens auf der Ausstellung des Britischen Weltreiches in Wembley, London. Oder mit Patrick Chalmers' Worten: „Was wir auf dem Karussell verlieren, gewinnen wir wieder auf der Schaukel."

Pentecôte 1924. Les joies et les terreurs du manège à l'Exposition de l'Empire britannique, Wembley, Londres. Comme le disait Patrick Chalmers : « Ce que l'on perd dans les manèges, on le retrouve dans les balançoires ».

January 1926. A rare fall of snow in Hyde Park, London. This time the two smokers are the Misses Debenham, and this is no *après ski* cigarette – they have yet to take their exercise.

Januar 1926. Seltener Schnee im Londoner Hyde Park. Die Debenham-Töchter rauchen keine Après-Ski-Zigarette, denn die sportliche Betätigung steht ihnen noch bevor.

Janvier 1926. Le Hyde Park à Londres sous la neige, c'est rare. Ces deux femmes sont les demoiselles Debenham, fumant une cigarette, mais avant de chausser leurs skis.

'Home is the hunter, home from the hill...' – and home from the kill in this case. The scene is a field in Devon, England: the time, July 1926.

„Heim kehrt der Jäger, heim von der Pirsch ..." – die offensichtlich erfolgreich verlaufen ist. Schauplatz war ein Feld in Devon im Juli 1926.

« Le chasseur est de retour, descendu de la colline... » avec, en l'occurrence, un butin. La scène se déroule sur un champ de Devon, Angleterre, en juillet 1926.

5. Entertainment
Unterhaltung
Divertissements

The Charleston Age. It was the dance that personified the Twenties: at once jazzy, witty, light-hearted, athletic, sexy and mischievous.

Die Zeit des Charleston. Er war der Inbegriff der zwanziger Jahre: wild, verschmitzt, unbeschwert, aber auch sportlich und erotisch.

L'époque du charleston. Cette danse résume à elle seule les années vingt: jazzique, drôle, légère, athlétique, sexy et coquine.

5. Entertainment
Unterhaltung
Divertissements

So many new words entered the vocabulary in the Twenties, almost all of them from the world of entertainment: 'It', 'flapper', 'talkies', 'Charleston' (and a dozen other dances). It was perhaps the one decade where artistically everything seemed to be better than ever before.

Silent movies reached their peak in the slapstick of Buster Keaton, Harry Langdon, Laurel and Hardy, and Charlie Chaplin; in the dramas of Sergei Eisenstein, King Vidor, and Erich von Stroheim; in the charming comedies of René Clair, Frank Capra, and Ernst Lubitsch. Ravel, Debussy, Stravinsky and Prokofiev produced orchestral, symphonic and chamber works that ranked with the finest. King Oliver, Bix Beiderbecke, Jelly Roll Morton and a young Duke Ellington wrote, played, and thankfully recorded, some of the greatest jazz of all time.

Prohibition did as little to curb people's enjoyment of life as it did to cut down their supply of alcohol. Everybody danced, everywhere – in clubs and dance halls, at home and in the streets, at charity balls and in non-stop competitions, in chorus lines and couples. And such dances! The Bunny Hug, the Black Bottom, the Drag, the Wob-a-ly Walk, the Kickaboo…

'Though the Jazz Age continued,' wrote Scott Fitzgerald, 'it became less and less an affair of youth.' Nobody chronicled it better than Fitzgerald.

In den zwanziger Jahren entstanden zahlreiche neue Wörter, die fast alle aus dem Bereich der Unterhaltung stammten: „It“ (Sex-Appeal), „flapper“ (modebewußtes Mädchen), „talkies“ (Tonfilme), „Charleston“ (und ein Dutzend anderer Tänze). Es war vielleicht das einzige Jahrzehnt, in dem im künstlerischen Bereich alles besser schien als je zuvor.

Der Stummfilm erreichte seinen Höhepunkt mit Slapstick-Filmen mit Buster Keaton, Harry Langdon, Laurel und Hardy und Charlie Chaplin, mit den dramatischen Filmen von Sergej Eisenstein, King Vidor und Erich von Stroheim und mit den charmanten Komödien von René

Clair, Frank Capra und Ernst Lubitsch. Ravel, Debussy, Strawinsky und Prokofjew komponierten wunderbare Orchesterwerke, Kammermusik und Symphonien. King Oliver, Bix Beiderbecke, Jelly Roll Morton und der junge Duke Ellington komponierten und spielten zeitlosen, großartigen Jazz, der glücklicherweise in Studioaufnahmen erhalten blieb.

Die Prohibition hinderte die Menschen weder daran, ihr Leben zu genießen noch Alkoholkonsum einzuschränken. Jedermann tanzte und zwar überall: in Clubs und Tanzsälen, zu Hause und auf der Straße, auf Wohltätigkeitsbällen und bei Wettbewerben im Marathontanzen, in Gruppen und zu zweit. Und was für Tänze! Der Bunny Hug, den Black Bottom, der Drag, der Wob-a-ly Walk, der Kickaboo…

„Obwohl das Zeitalter des Jazz andauerte", schrieb Scott Fitzgerald, „hatte es immer weniger etwas mit Jugend zu tun." Niemand schilderte diese Zeit genauer als Fitzgerald.

Un grand nombre de mots nouveaux firent leur apparition dans les années vingt, presque tous issus du monde du spectacle, dont « It » pour sexy, « flapper » pour jeune fille délurée, « talkies » pour cinéma parlant, « charleston » (et une dizaine d'autres noms de danses). Ce fut peut-être la seule décennie durant laquelle, d'un point de vue artistique, tout semblait mieux qu'avant.

Ce fut l'apogée des films muets avec les comédies de Buster Keaton, Harry Langdon, Laurel et Hardy et Charlie Chaplin, les drames de Serge Eisenstein, King Vidor et Erich von Stroheim ou les comédies légères de René Clair, Frank Capra et Ernst Lubitsch. Les compositions de Ravel, Debussy, Stravinski et Prokofiev comptent parmi les plus belles symphonies et musiques de chambre ou pour orchestre. King Oliver, Bix Beiderbecke, Jelly Roll Morton et le jeune Duke Ellington composèrent, interprétèrent et, heureusement, enregistrèrent des morceaux d'anthologie de l'histoire du jazz.

La prohibition n'empêcha ni les gens de s'amuser ni diminua leur consommation d'alcool. Tout le monde dansait, n'importe où – dans les boîtes de nuit et les salles de bal, à la maison et dans la rue, aux galas de charité et dans les concours de danse, en groupes et par deux. Et quelles danses ! Il y avait le Bunny hug, le Black Bottom, le Wob-a-ly Walk, le Drag, le Kickaboo…

« L'age du jazz n'était pas terminé », écrivait Scott Fitzgerald, « mais c'était de moins en moins une affaire de jeunesse ». Personne n'a su mieux que lui résumer l'état d'esprit de cette époque.

The 'It' girl, Clara Bow, on Malibu Beach, 1927. Bob, bangles, Cupid's bow lips – she personified the Twenties.

Clara Bow verkörperte in den zwanziger Jahren den Sex-Appeal schlechthin, Malibu, 1927. Auf dieser Aufnahme posiert sie mit lockigem Kurzhaarschnitt und Kußmund am Strand.

Sur une plage de Malibu, 1927. Coupe au carré et bouche en cœur, Clara Bow incarne parfaitement la fille sexy des années vingt.

Louise Brooks, on a trapeze in her Hollywood home, 1925. Her sex appeal was challenging, her aura tragic.

Louise Brooks auf einem Trapez in ihrem Haus in Hollywood, 1925. Ihr Sex-Appeal war provokativ, ihre Aura eher tragisch.

Louise Brooks, sur un trapèze dans sa maison de Hollywood, 1925. Son sex-appeal était irrésistible, son aura tragique.

Anna Pavlova (right) and Mary Pickford on the set of *The Thief of Bagdad*, Hollywood, 1924. Neither was in the film.

Anna Pawlowa (rechts) und Mary Pickford während der Dreharbeiten zu *Der Dieb von Bagdad*, Hollywood, 1924. Weder die eine noch die andere waren in dem Film zu bewundern.

Anna Pavlova (à droite) et Mary Pickford lors du tournage du *Voleur de Bagdad*, Hollywood, 1924. Ni l'une ni l'autre n'apparaissent dans le film.

Brother and sister, Fred and Adele Austerlitz – better known as the Astaires, June 1923. They are dancing on the roof of the Savoy Hotel, London. They appeared in a musical called *Stop Flirting*, and Britain fell in love with them.

Bruder und Schwester, Fred und Adele Austerlitz – besser bekannt als die Astairs, Juni 1923 Sie tanzen auf dem Dach des Londoner Savoy Hotels. Als sie mit dem Musical *Stop Flirting* gastierten, war das britische Publikum von ihnen hingerissen.

Frère et sœur. Fred et Adèle Austerlitz – plus connus sous le nom d'Astaire, juin 1923. Ils dansant sur le toit de l'hôtel Savoy, Londres. Ils jouèrent dans *Stop Flirting*, une comédie musicale, et conquirent le cœur de tous les Britanniques.

A very young James Cagney poses on a Hollywood diving board in the late Twenties. He made his film debut in 1928.

Der junge James Cagney posiert Ende der zwanziger Jahre auf einem Sprungbrett in Hollywood. 1928 hatte er seinen ersten Filmauftritt.

Le très jeune James Cagney posant sur un plongeoir à Hollywood à la fin des années vingt. Son premier film date de 1928.

Bebe Daniels and her husband, Ben Lyon, at their beach house in California. Daniels starred in many silent films, but her big break came in an early 'talkie' called *Rio Rita*. Ben Lyon's greatest success was still to come, in *Hell's Angels*.

Bebe Daniels mit ihrem Ehemann, Ben Lyon, in ihrem Strandhaus in Kalifornien. Daniels war bereits ein Stummfilmstar, doch der große Durchbruch gelang ihr mit einem der ersten Tonfilme, *Rio Rita*. Auch Ben Lyons größter Erfolg stand noch bevor, in *Engel der Hölle*.

Bebe Daniels et son mari, Ben Lyon, dans leur propriété aux bords de la mer, en Californie. Daniels joua dans beaucoup de films muets, mais fut révélée dans *Rio Rita*, un des premiers films parlants. Ben Lyon deviendrait célèbre avec *Les Anges de l'Enfer*.

The Race to stardom. Greta Garbo gets set to take Hollywood by storm, 1927. She had arrived from Sweden the year before.

Auf dem Weg zum Ruhm. Greta Garbo schickt sich an, Hollywood im Sturm zu erobern, 1927. Erst ein Jahr zuvor hatte sie Schweden verlassen.

En piste pour la gloire. Greta Garbo, prête à faire des ravages à Hollywood, 1927. Elle était arrivée de Suède l'année précédente.

Marlene Dietrich snuggles into the comforts of Hollywood, 1929. She was already a great star in Germany, where she had made many films and many fans. 'I can only say that she makes reason totter on her throne,' wrote film critic James Agate.

Marlene Dietrich genießt die Annehmlichkeiten Hollywoods, 1929. In Deutschland, wo sie zahlreiche Filme gedreht hatte und zahlreiche Anhänger besaß, war sie bereits ein Star. „Ich kann nur sagen, daß sie die Vernunft ins Wanken bringt", schrieb der Filmkritiker James Agate.

Marlène Dietrich, profite du confort d'Hollywood, 1929. Déjà une très grande vedette en Allemagne, où elle avait joué dans beaucoup de films, elle comptait de nombreux admirateurs. « Tout ce que je peux dire, c'est qu'elle défie la raison », déclara le critique de films James Agate.

A publicity montage of the silent film comedian Harry Langdon, 1926. Langdon's trade mark was his baby face, the outward manifestation of the sublimely naive character he played.

Eine Fotomontage zu Werbezwecken mit dem Stummfilmkomiker Harry Langdon, 1926. Langdons Markenzeichen war sein Milchgesicht, das äußere Merkmal der ergreifend naiven Figur, die er spielte.

Montage publicitaire pour le film muet du comique Harry Langdon, 1926. Langdon était facile à reconnaître avec sa tête de bébé, signe extérieur du personnage naïf qu'il jouait comme personne d'autre.

British movies at their passionate best, on a wind swept beach near Brighton, 1926. The film being made is *The Thrill*, a masterpiece that has totally disappeared from the cinematic world.

Der britische Film, wie er leidenschaftlicher nicht sein könnte, an einem windigen Strand in der Nähe von Brighton, 1926. Der Film, der hier gedreht wird, heißt *The Thrill*, ein Meisterwerk, das heute aus der Kinowelt verschwunden ist.

La passion selon le cinéma britannique sur une plage balayée par le vent, près de Brighton, 1926. Tournage de *The Thrill*, un chef-d'œuvre complètement oublié du monde du cinéma.

Twenty-three-year-old Walt Disney, 1924. The film in production here was *Peculiar Penguins*, an early Silly Symphony. Mickey Mouse was still four years away.

Der 23jährige Walt Disney, 1924. Hier bei Dreharbeiten zu *Peculiar Penguins*, einem frühen Film der Silly Symphony-Reihe. Mickey Mouse sollte erst vier Jahre später entstehen.

Walt Disney, âgé de 23 ans, 1924. Ici pendant le tournage de *Peculiar Penguins*, un des premiers de la série Silly Symphony. Quatre ans plus tard naissait Mickey Mouse.

Child actor Jackie Cooper signs for Louis B Mayer and MGM, 1928. Mayer's faith in Cooper was to pay off three years later, when he made *The Champ*, with Wallace Beery as the washed-up boxer.

Kinderdarsteller Jackie Cooper unterschreibt seinen Vertrag mit Louis B. Mayer und MGM, 1928. Das Vertrauen, das Mayer in Cooper hatte, sollte sich drei Jahre später auszahlen, als er mit Wallace Beery als erfolglosem Boxer den Film *The Champ* drehte.

Le jeune acteur Jackie Cooper signe un contrat avec Louis B. Mayer et la MGM, 1928. L'espoir qu'avait placé Mayer en Cooper serait récompensé trois ans plus tard, lorsqu'il tourna *The Champ*, avec Wallace Beery dans le rôle du boxeur en fin de carrière.

Lillian Gish, 1923. She was the ultimate in tragic heroines in such films as *Orphans of the Storm*, *The White Sister* and *La Bohème*.

Lillian Gish, 1923. Sie galt als die tragische Heldin schlechthin in Filmen wie *Waisen des Sturms*, *Die weiße Schwester* und *La Bohème*.

Lillian Gish, 1923. Elle fut une admirable tragédienne, notamment dans *Les deux orphelines*, *La sœur blanche* et *La Bohème*.

Guys and Dolls. Charlie Chaplin admires a puppet version of the 'Little Fella', the character he played in almost all his comedies.

Männer und Puppen. Charlie Chaplin bewundert eine Puppenversion des kleinen Burschen, den er in fast all seinen komischen Filmen verkörperte.

L'homme et sa marionnette. Charlie Chaplin admire un minuscule Charlot, personnage qu'il joua dans la plupart de ses comédies.

Buster Keaton with his *alter ego*, given to him by a German woodcarver, 1928. The great days of Keaton's career were already over.

Buster Keaton mit seinem Alter ego, das ihm ein deutscher Holzschnitzer geschenkt hatte, 1928. Seine große Zeit war bereits vorüber.

Buster Keaton et son double, offert par un sculpteur allemand, 1928. Les jours de gloire étaient déjà passés pour Keaton.

Mack Sennett's Keystone Kops at the height of their popularity, 1920. Sennett had wanted to be an opera singer, but he started in films in 1908. He was the man who 'discovered' Chaplin and Fatty Arbuckle, and altered the face of American screen comedy.

Mack Sennetts Keystone Kops, auf der Höhe ihrer Popularität, 1920. Ursprünglich wollte Sennett Opernsänger werden, 1908 spielte er jedoch seine erste Filmrolle. Er „entdeckte" Chaplin und Fatty Arbuckle und nahm entscheidenden Einfluß auf die amerikanischen Filmkomödie.

Les Keystone Kops de Mack Sennett, au sommet de leur popularité, 1920. Sennett aurait voulu être chanteur d'opéra mais débuta au cinéma en 1908. Il « découvrit » Chaplin et Fatty Arbuckle et créa un style de comédie qui allait changer le cinéma américain.

A regular and reliable gag – Harold Lloyd loses his car in a scene from *Girl Shy*, 1924. It was one of Lloyd's most successful films financially, one of the year's top five money-makers. Predictably, it ended in a chase, with Lloyd on top of a runaway streetcar.

Ein immer wieder gerne verwendeter Filmgag – Harold Lloyds Wagen stürzt in *Mädchenscheu* in den Abgrund, 1924. Er wurde zum Kassenschlager und gehörte zu den fünf bestbesuchten Filmen jenes Jahres. Wie zu erwarten, endete der Film mit einer Verfolgungsjagd, in der sich Lloyd allerdings auf dem Dach einer führerlosen Straßenbahn befand.

Un gag sûr – Harold Lloyd perd sa voiture dans une scène de *Girl Shy*, 1924. Ce film, un des plus grands succès commerciaux de Lloyd, figura parmi les cinq films en tête du box-office de cette année-là. Il se termine par une infaillible poursuite avec Lloyd sur le toit d'un tramway lancé à folle allure.

Erich von Stroheim in the Twenties. As an actor he was billed as 'The Man You Love to Hate'.

Erich von Stroheim in den zwanziger Jahren. Als Schauspieler kündigte man ihn auf Plakaten als „den Mann, den man gerne haßt“ an.

Erich von Stroheim dans les années vingt. En tant qu'acteur, il incarnait « l'homme qu'on adore détester ».

Douglas Fairbanks on the set of *The Gaucho*, 1928. Many consider it was his best film, perhaps because he didn't direct it. The director was F Richard Jones, who managed to curtail some of Fairbanks's over-exuberant swashbuckling.

Douglas Fairbanks bei den Dreharbeiten zu *Der Gaucho*, 1928. Viele Cineasten halten diesen Film für seinen besten, vielleicht weil er ausnahmsweise nicht selbst Regie führte, sondern F. Richard Jones. Diesem gelang es, Fairbanks' überschwenglich verwegenen Darstellungsstil zu zügeln.

Douglas Fairbanks lors du tournage de *The Gaucho*, 1928. Il est considéré par beaucoup comme son meilleur film, peut-être parce que ce ne fut pas lui qui en signa la mise en scène mais F. Richard Jones. Ce dernier réussit à écourter les scènes sur-jouées de cape et d'épée de Fairbanks.

Preparing to go in front of the camera. MGM star Gwen Lee uses a reflector as a mirror while she applies her make-up, 1929.

Vorbereitungen vor den Filmaufnahmen. MGM-Star Gwen Lee verwendet einen Reflektor als Spiegel, um ihr Make-up zu korrigieren, 1929.

Préparatifs avant le tournage. Gwen Lee, actrice vedette de la MGM, se sert d'un projecteur comme miroir pour se maquiller, 1929.

The camera goes in front. A cameraman stands on the footplate of the London to Carlisle Express, 1924. The industry was rapidly becoming technically more ambitious.

Die Kamera an vorderster Front. Ein Kameramann filmt von der Plattform eines Schnellzuges der Strecke London-Carlisle, 1924. Die Filmindustrie entwickelte sehr rasch großen technischen Ehrgeiz.

La caméra passe au premier plan. Un caméraman installé à l'avant de l'Express Londres-Carlisle, 1924. L'industrie cinématographique accomplissait des prouesses techniques toujours plus étonnantes.

Matinée idols. Noel Coward at the height of his early fame in the late Twenties – 'My stock that winter was obstinately high.'

Matinée-Idole. Noel Coward auf der Höhe seines frühen Erfolges in den späten zwanziger Jahren. „Mein Kurswert blieb in jenem Winter hartnäckig oben."

L'idole du public féminin. Noel Coward au sommet de sa gloire qui commença à la fin des années vingt. « Ma cote est restée cet hiver-là abstinément haute. »

Ivor Novello – actor, composer, director and night club owner – as Pierre Boucheron in *The Rat*, 1924.

Ivor Novello – Schauspieler, Komponist, Regisseur und Nachtclubbesitzer in der Rolle des Pierre Boucheron in *Die Ratte*, 1924.

Ivor Novello – acteur, compositeur, metteur en scène et propriétaire d'une boîte de nuit – incarne Pierre Boucheron dans *Le Rat*, 1924.

Percival Mackey's Band 'get hot' on the roof of the London Palladium, 1927. The dancer is Monti Ryan, an actress married to Mackey.

Percival Mackeys Tanzkapelle „swingen" auf dem Dach des Londoner Palladium, 1927. Die Tänzerin ist die Schauspielerin Monti Ryan, Mackeys Ehefrau.

Percival Mackey et son orchestre « font un bœuf » sur le toit du Palladium à Londres, 1927. La danseuse est l'actrice Monti Ryan, – femme de Mackey.

His Master's Voice – Paul Robeson, 1925. Robeson first qualified as a lawyer before becoming perhaps the most famous singer of all time. His glorious bass voice was first recorded early in the Twenties, and by the time this photograph was taken, he had starred on Broadway and in London's West End.

Die Stimme seines Herrn – Paul Robeson, 1925. Bevor er zum bekanntesten Sänger aller Zeiten avancierte, war Paul Robeson Anwalt. Seine herrliche Baßstimme wurde erstmals zu Beginn der zwanziger Jahre aufgenommen. Als diese Fotografie entstand, war Robeson bereits am Broadway und im Londoner West End aufgetreten.

La « voix de son maître » – Paul Robeson, 1925. Avocat de métier, Robeson devint l'un des chanteurs les plus connus de tous les temps. Son premier enregistrement date du début des années vingt. A l'époque où fut prise cette photographie, il s'était déjà produit à Broadway et dans le West End à Londres.

The Five Aces, 1925. The peculiar-looking violin has a horn attachment to increase volume in a noisy dance hall.

Die Five Aces, 1925. Die ungewöhnlich anmutende Geige hatte einen Hornaufsatz, damit sie im Lärm eines Tanzsaales noch zu hören war.

Les Five Aces, 1925. Cet étrange violon est pourvu d'un cor pour amplifier le son dans les salles de bal bruyantes.

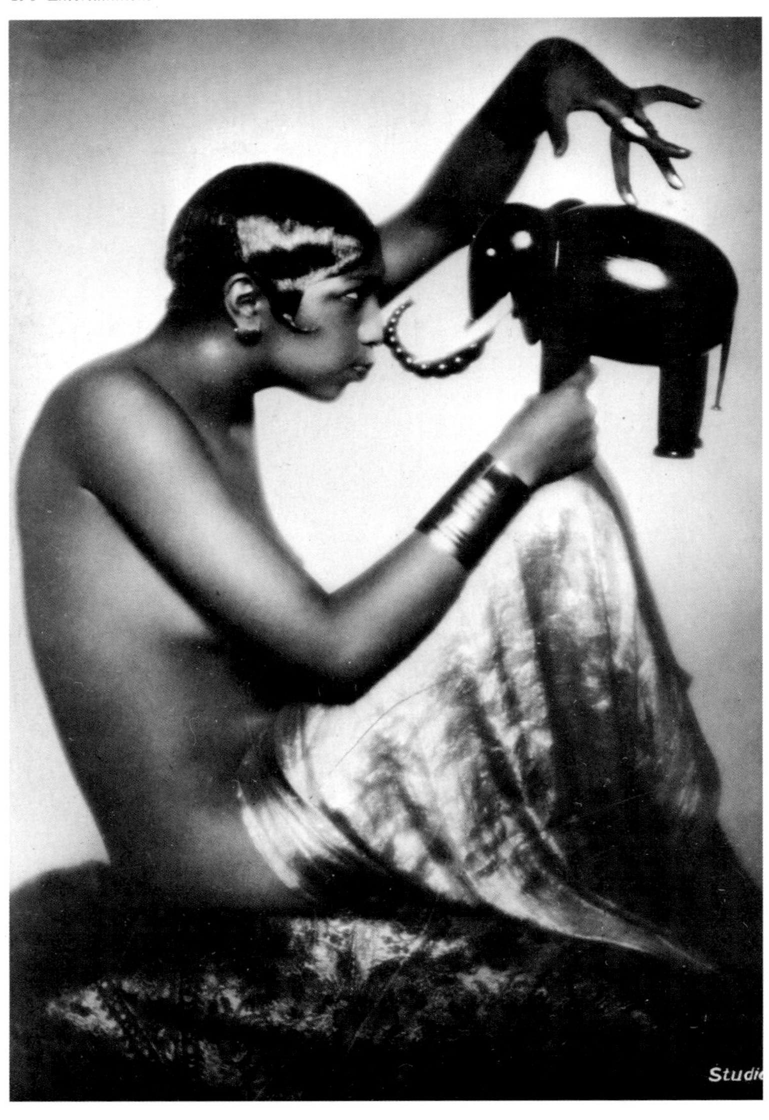

The American cabaret star Josephine Baker, 1920. Baker delighted European audiences during the Twenties. 'She dances for hours without the slightest trace of tiredness' – Harry Kessler, Berlin 1926.

Der amerikanische Varieté-Star Josephine Baker, 1920. In den zwanziger Jahren begeisterte die Baker auch das europäische Publikum. „Sie tanzte stundenlang, ohne auch nur die geringsten Anzeichen von Ermüdung zu zeigen“, Harry Kessler, Berlin, 1926

La reine du cabaret, l'Américaine Joséphine Baker, 1920. Baker séduisit le public européen des années vingt. « Elle peut danser des heures sans montrer le moindre signe de fatigue », Harry Kessler, Berlin, 1926.

The Folies-Bergère, Paris, February 1929. Originally, the Folies was an opera house; by the Twenties it had become a famous music hall. This was the heyday of such stars as Mistinguett and Maurice Chevalier.

Die Folies-Bergère, Paris, Februar 1929. Das ehemalige Opernhaus hatte sich in den zwanziger Jahren zu einem berühmten Varieté-Theater entwickelt, in dem Stars wie Mistinguett und Maurice Chevalier ihre Glanzzeit erlebten.

Les Folies-Bergère, Paris, février 1929. Ce bâtiment fut un opéra avant de devenir, dans les années vingt, un célèbre music-hall. Ce fut la grande époque des vedettes comme Mistinguett et Maurice Chevalier.

Dame Laura Knight sketches chorus girls behind the scenes at Olympia, West London, 1929. The girls were performing in the circus which traditionally came to Olympia every winter. Many routines for chorus lines owed as much to acrobatics as to dancing in the Twenties.

Dame Laura Knight zeichnet Revuetänzerinnen hinter den Kulissen des Olympia, West London, 1929. Die Tänzerinnen gehören einem Zirkus an, der jeden Winter im Olympia gastierte. Für die Auftritte in den zwanziger Jahren waren ebenso akrobatische wie tänzerische Einlagen charakteristisch.

Dame Laura Knight fait le portrait de danseuses dans les coulisses de l'Olympia, Londres-Ouest, 1929. Les danseuses faisaient partie du cirque qui, selon la tradition, s'installait chaque hiver à l'Olympia. A cette époque, la plupart des numéros étaient un mélange d'acrobaties et de danse.

March 1928. The Tiller Girls at the London Plaza. The Tiller Girls were the most famous chorus line in Britain between the wars, noted for the precision of their high-kicking routines.

März 1928. Die Tiller Girls im Londoner Plaza. Diese Revuetänzerinnen waren für die Präzision ihrer Darbietung berühmt und blieben in der Zeit zwischen den Weltkriegen die bekannteste Tanztruppe Großbritanniens.

Mars 1928. La troupe des Tiller Girls au Plaza de Londres. Cette troupe, connue pour ses numéros de grande précision, fut la plus célèbre de Grande-Bretagne pendant l'entre-deux-guerres.

The Alfred Jackson Dancing Girls, London, June 1928. The choreography may owe more to the Health and Fitness Movement, but audiences were always delighted by the performance.

Die Alfred Jackson Dancing Girls, London, Juni 1928. Ihre Choreographie schien zwar eher auf die Gesundheits- und Fitneßbewegung zurückzugehen, aber das Publikum war von ihren Darbietungen begeistert.

Les Alfred Jackson Dancing Girls, Londres, juin 1928. La chorégraphie tient plus de la gymnastique que de la danse, mais le public adorait ce genre de numéro.

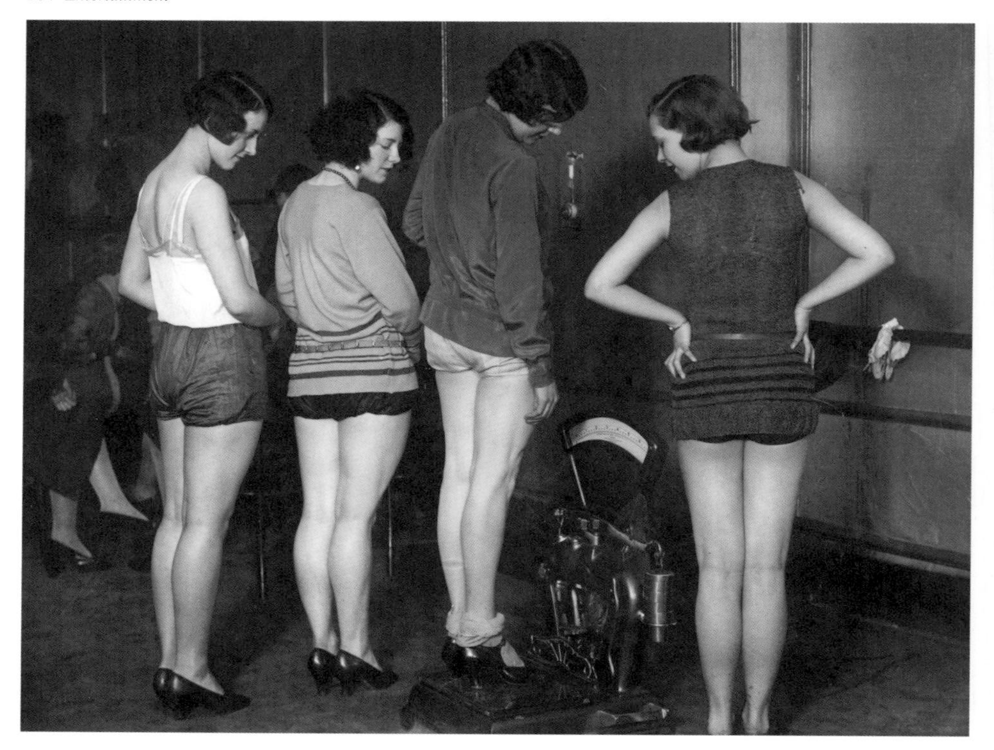

Four of C B Cochran's "Young Ladies" check their weight, 1925. Cochran was a theatrical impresario, famous for staging musicals and revues. To be selected as one of his Young Ladies was the ambition of thousands of women from all classes.

Vier von C. B. Cochrans „Young Ladies" prüfen ihr Gewicht, 1925. Theaterdirektor Cochran war bekannt für seine Musicals und Revuen. Tausende von Frauen aus allen gesellschaftlichen Schichten träumten davon, zum Kreis seiner Young Ladies zu gehören.

Quatre « Young Ladies » de la troupe de C. B. Cochran contrôlent leur poids, 1925. Cochran était un impresario connu pour ses comédies musicales et ses revues. Des milliers de femmes, toutes classes confondues, rêvaient de devenir l'une de ses Young Ladies.

A typical theatrical dressing room for chorus girls, 1925. It was a tough life, though there was always the hope that some 'Stage Door Johnny' would be waiting at the end of the show to whisk you away to a champagne supper and an honest proposal.

Eine typische Theatergarderobe für Revuetänzerinnen, 1925. Es war ein hartes Leben. Dennoch gaben viele der Mädchen die Hoffnung nicht auf, daß eines Abends nach dem Auftritt ein vornehmer Herr am Bühneneingang warten würde, um sie mit ehrenvollen Absichten zu einem Champagner-Diner zu entführen.

Scène classique dans une loge de danseuses, 1925. Leur vie était dure mais il y avait toujours l'espoir qu'un soir, après le spectacle, un homme vous attende à l'entrée des artistes pour inviter à dîner au champagne et vous faire une offre sérieuse.

The 'hands on knees crossover' step from the most famous and enduring dance of the Twenties – the Charleston. The monkey was not obligatory.

Der Kreuzgriff-Schritt des legendären Tanzes der zwanziger Jahre – der Charleston. Der Affe gehörte nicht zum Pflichtprogramm.

Mains croisées sur les genoux, le fameux pas de charleston qui fut la danse la plus célèbre des années vingt. La présence du singe était facultative.

Arimand Banu, Indian dancer and snake charmer, 1925. Banu's erotic and exotic dancing, partnered by a cobra, understandably astonished British audiences.

Arimand Banu, indische Tänzerin und Schlangenbeschwörerin, 1925. Ihre sowohl exotische als auch erotische Darbietung, mit einer Kobra als Partnerin, verblüffte verständlicherweise das britische Publikum.

Arimand Banu, danseuse et charmeuse de serpent indienne, 1925. Cette danse érotique et exotique, exécutée avec un cobra, impressionnait le public britannique.

A vision of ancient Greece, 1924. Isadora Duncan and her followers breathed fresh air into dance during the Twenties. Duncan founded schools of dance in Berlin, Vienna, Salzburg and Moscow.

Eine Vision des antiken Griechenland, 1924. Isadora Duncan gründete in den zwanziger Jahren Tanzschulen in Berlin, Wien, Salzburg und Moskau und brachte mit ihren Schülerinnen frischen Wind in den Tanz.

Vision de la Grèce antique, 1924. Isadora Duncan et ses disciples apportèrent dans les années vingt un souffle nouveau à la danse. Duncan fonda des écoles de danse à Berlin, Vienne, Salzbourg et Moscou.

A giant leap for womankind... Three Marion Morgan dancers bend their backs for the sake of their art, 1926.

Ein riesiger Sprung für die Frauen ... Drei Tänzerinnen der Gruppe von Marion Morgan verbiegen sich um der Kunst willen den Rücken, 1926.

Pas de géant pour la cause des femmes... Trois danseuses du groupe de Marion Morgan combrant le dos au nom de la danse, 1926.

June 1926. Ladies of the lake. Students from the Mayfair School of Dancing reveal their talents in the Royal Botanic Gardens, Regent's Park, London.

Juni 1926. Die Damen vom See. Elevinnen der Tanzschule von Mayfair zeigen ihr Talent im Botanischen Garten des Londoner Regent's Park.

Juin 1926. Les Dames du lac. Des élèves de l'Ecole de danse de Mayfair font étalage de leurs talents au jardin botanique de Regent's Park, Londres.

Heading for stardom, 1928. A Parisian dancer strikes a symmetrical, but not very attractive, pose.

Auf dem Weg zum Ruhm, 1928. Eine Pariser Tänzerin in einer zwar symmetrischen, jedoch nicht sehr anmutigen Position.

Envol vers la gloire, 1928. Cette danseuse parisienne prend une pose symétriquement parfaite mais guère séduisante.

December 1926. The essential steps of the 'Kickaboo'. Many of the dances introduced in the Twenties had very short lives. One minute they were 'all the rage' or 'the berries', the next they were as out of date as the two-step.

Dezember 1926. Die wichtigsten Schritte des „Kickaboo". Viele Tänze der zwanziger Jahre waren nur kurze Zeit „in". Eben machten sie noch Furore, um im nächsten Augenblick so altmodisch zu sein wie der Pas de deux.

Décembre 1926. Les pas de base du « kickaboo ». La plupart des danses inventées dans les années vingt ne duraient pas. A peine avaient-elles fait fureur qu'elles étaient aussi démodées que le pas de deux.

A couple dance the Charleston in a scene from the stage musical *Just a Kiss* at the Shaftesbury Theatre, London, 1926.

Ein Paar tanzt den Charleston in einer Szene des Musicals *Just a kiss* am Shaftesbury Theatre, London, 1926.

Un couple dansant le charleston dans une comédie musicale intitulée *Just a Kiss* au Shaftesbury Theatre, Londres, 1926.

January 1925. Novelty night at the East Ham Palais de Danse. This competition took the form of a crossword puzzle, the clues to which were given in the different types of dance played by the band.

Januar 1925. Die Nacht der Neuheiten im Tanzpalast von East Ham. Dieser Wettbewerb war eine Art Kreuzworträtsel, dessen Lösungen sich aus den verschiedenen Tänzen ergaben, die die Kapelle anstimmte.

Janvier 1925. Soirée des nouveautés au Palais de danse de East Ham. Le concours était une sorte de mots croisés dont les réponses étaient données par les différentes danses jouées par l'orchestre.

How to dance the Charleston, in six easy steps, 1925. It took the Twenties by storm – if you didn't Charleston, you were a social outcast.

Sechs einfache Schritte, um den Charleston zu tanzen, 1925. Dieser Tanz eroberte die zwanziger Jahre im Sturm – wer ihn nicht beherrschte, galt als gesellschaftlicher Außenseiter.

Six pas faciles pour danser le charleston, 1925. Cette danse connut un succès foudroyant dans les années vingt – si vous ne saviez pas danser le charleston, vous n'étiez rien, socialement parlant.

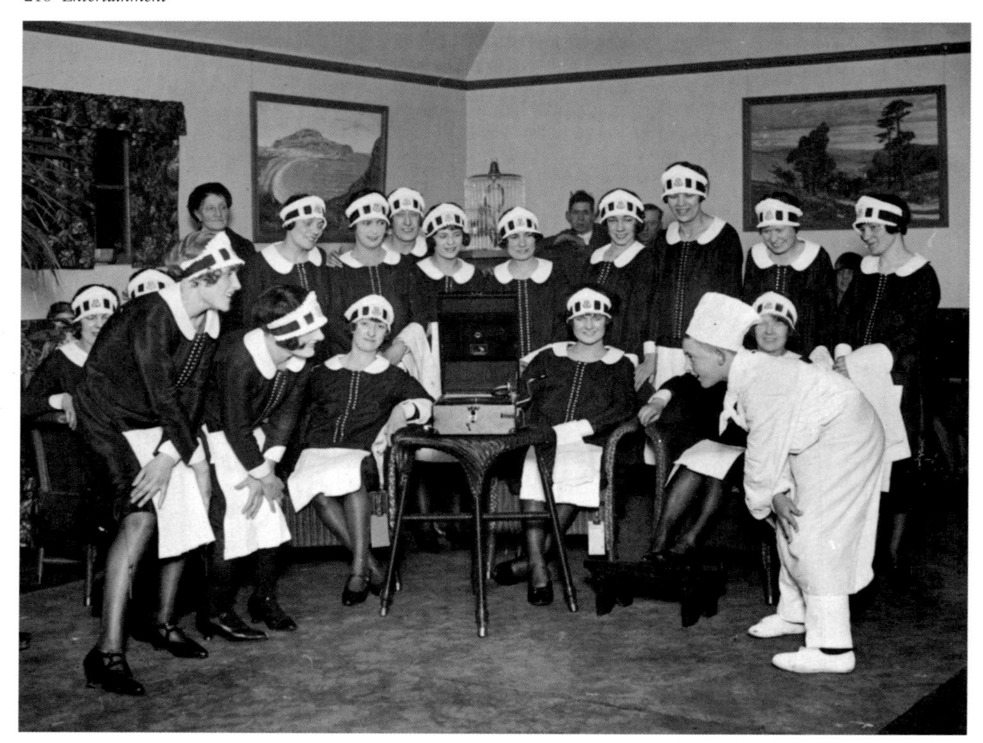

'Black Bottom, a new rhythm, it's sure gottem...' An attentive crowd of nippies (waitresses) watch a junior chef demonstrate the Black Bottom in the rest room of one of the Lyon's Corner Houses, London, 1927.

„Black Bottom, ein neuer Rhythmus, der einen mitreißt ..." Ein junger Koch zeigt den aufmerksamen Serviererinnen den Black Bottom im Hinterzimmer eines Restaurantes der Kette Lyon's, London, 1927.

« Black bottom, un nouveau rythme qui vous prend... » Ces serveuses assistent avec attention à une démonstration de Black Bottom, donnée par un jeune cuisinier dans l'arrière-salle d'un restaurant de la chaîne Lyon's Corner House, Londres, 1927.

According to the words of the song, the Charleston was 'made in Carolina'. It had travelled a long way by the time these hardy couples danced it in the snow, clad only in their underwear, 1927.

Einem Lied zufolge stammt der Charleston aus Carolina. Bis ihn diese abgehärteten Paare – nur mit Unterwäsche bekleidet – im Schnee tanzten, hatte er demnach einen weiten Weg zurückgelegt, 1927.

A en croire les paroles de la chanson, le charleston fut « inventé en Caroline ». Il avait fait un bon bout de chemin avant que ces couples courageux le dansent dans la neige, vêtus de simples sous-vêtements, 1927.

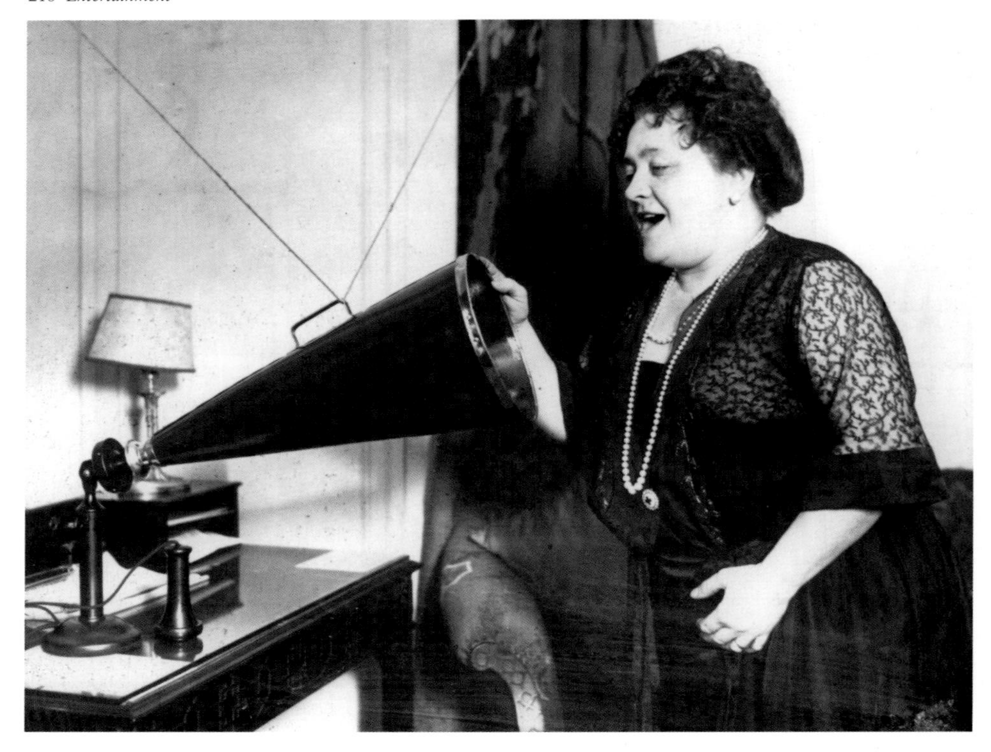

The famous Italian coloratura soprano, Luisa Tetrazzini, 1921. The diva was by then 50 years old, but still in good voice. Although the recording apparatus is primitive, it brought the voices of the great to millions of households.

Die berühmte italienische Koloratursopranistin Luisa Tetrazzini, 1921. Selbst mit 50 Jahren hatte die Diva noch eine einmalige Stimme. Obwohl das Aufnahmegerät recht einfach war, übermittelte es den Gesang der Großen in Millionen Haushalte.

La célèbre soprano italienne, Luisa Tetrazzini, 1921. A 50 ans, la diva avait encore une belle voix. Les méthodes d'enregistrement, alors primitives, permirent néanmoins à des millions de gens de découvrir les grands chanteurs de l'époque.

The mulit-instrumentalist Teddy Brown plays a serenade on his saxophone. Brown originally played with the New York Philharmonic Orchestra, but found more fund and money in dance bands and on the stage. In the Twenties, his was the resident band at London's Café de Paris.

Der Multi-Instrumentalist Teddy Brown spielt ein Ständchen auf seinem Saxophon. Brown war ursprünglich Mitglied des New York Philharmonic Orchestra. Bald stellte er aber fest, daß das Spiel in Tanzkapellen und auf der Bühne amüsanter und einträglicher war. In den zwanziger Jahren war seine Band die hauseigene Tanzkapelle des Londoner Café de Paris.

Teddy Brown, multi-instrumentiste, joue une sérénade au saxophone. Il fit ses débuts à l'Orchestre philharmonique de New York mais, préférant la variété et l'argebt, il travailla pour des orchestres de bal et se produisit sur scène. Dans les années vingt, il s'installa avec son orchestre au Café de Paris à Londres.

6. Fashion and the arts
Mode und die schönsten Künste
La mode et les arts

Santa Proud fashions, 1928. One of the features of clothes design in the Twenties is that, to modern eyes, it isn't always easy to distinguish the purpose for which the outfit was designed – Pyjamas? Beach-wear? Party? But the beauty cannot be denied.

Ein Santa Proud-Modell, 1928. Ein Charakteristikum der Zwanziger-Jahre-Mode war, daß man nicht immer gleich erkennen konnte, für welchen Zweck die jeweilige Kleidung entworfen worden war. Handelt es sich hier um einen Pyjama, um Strandmode oder Partygarderobe? Was immer es sein mag, es ist zweifellos elegant.

La mode selon Santa Proud, 1928. L'une des caractéristiques de la mode des années vingt est qu'il est parfois difficile de deviner la fonction du vêtement – pyjama ? tenue de plage ? tenue de soirée ? Mais l'élégance est indéniable.

6. Fashion and the arts
Mode und die schönsten Künste
La mode et les arts

Design in the Twenties was wild, extravagant, revolutionary and, much of it, extremely beautiful. Clothes were often outrageous – the vast Oxford bags (wider even than Seventies flares), the fat fur coat that made its wearer look like Bigfoot, the tight-fitting cloche hat, the low-slung waistline that reached below the buttocks.

However, the wardrobe of the Twenties is still immensely attractive. Women wore beautiful coats and stunning evening wear. The hemline crept up the leg as the decade unfolded, the back line dropped a little lower, but the neckline remained chaste and demure.

Men's clothes were sometimes fun, sometimes smart in a yachting-blazer-and-flannels way, but often little changed from what their fathers had worn. However, every young man, from Harold Lloyd to Al Capone and the Duke of Windsor, wore a boater or straw hat.

Art became increasingly like coloured geometry, from the abstract paintings of Miró and Mondrian, to the vibrant colours and strong patterns of the Bauhaus; from the Purist architecture of Le Corbusier to the sturdy sculptures of Epstein and Gill. It was an age of monuments: to the past, in war memorials everywhere; to the future, in skyscrapers and hydroelectric dams; and to the present, in picture palaces and monstrous factories.

Das Design der zwanziger Jahre war wild, extravagant, revolutionär und größtenteils wunderschön, die Kleidung oft recht ausgefallen. Es gab weitgeschnittene Oxford-Hosen (die sogar noch weiter waren als die ausgestellten Hosen der siebziger Jahre), dicke Pelzmäntel, die die Trägerinnen eher wie Yetis aussehen ließen, enganliegende Topfhüte und tief angesetzte Taillen, die unterhalb der Hüfte saßen.

Dennoch blieb die Mode der zwanziger Jahre ungeheuer attraktiv. Die Damen trugen sehr schöne Mäntel und atemberaubende Abendkleider. Der Saum kletterte im Laufe der Zeit nach oben, und der Rückenausschnitt nach unten. Der Halsausschnitt jedoch blieb weiterhin sittsam und spröde.

Die Herrenbekleidung war zum Teil leger, zum Teil elegant mit Blazer und Tuchhose, jedoch größtenteils kaum anders als bisher. Allerdings trug jeder junge Mann, von Harold Lloyd über Al Capone bis zum Herzog von Windsor, eine Kreissäge oder einen Strohhut.

In der Kunst begann Geometrie, die Szene zu beherrschen, von den abstrakten Gemälden Mirós und Mondrians bis zu den leuchtenden Farben und ausdrucksstarken Mustern des Bauhausstils, von der puristischen Architektur Le Corbusiers bis zu den kräftigen Skulpturen Epsteins und Gills. Es war auch das Zeitalter der Monumente: gewidmet der Vergangenheit in Form von Kriegsdenkmälern, der Zukunft in Form von Wolkenkratzern und Wasserkraftwerken und der Gegenwart in Form von Kinopalästen und riesigen Fabrikgebäuden.

Le design des années vingt fut osé, bizarre, révolutionnaire et, dans l'ensemble, extrêmement élégante. Les vêtements étaient souvent extravagants: les pantalons très amples dits « Oxford bags » (plus larges encore que les « pattes d'éléphant » des années soixante-dix), les épais manteaux de fourrure qui vous transformaient en yétis, les chapeaux-cloches très ajustés, les robes à la taille très basse.

Il n'empêche que la garde-robe de cette décennie plaît toujours autant. Les femmes portaient de magnifiques manteaux et des robes de soirée époustouflantes. Elles étaient plus courtes chaque année et l'encolure du dos s'ouvrait toujours davantage, tandis que le décolleté restait chaste et sage.

La mode masculine était parfois amusante, parfois élégante avec ses blazers et pantalons de flanelle style yacht mais, à vrai dire, elle ne se différenciait guère de celle que portait la génération précédente. Enfin, tous les jeunes gens, que ce soit Harold Lloyd, Al Capone ou le duc de Windsor, portaient des canotiers ou des chapeaux de paille.

L'art devenait une géométrie de couleurs – des peintures abstraites de Miró et Mondrian aux couleurs vibrantes et aux motifs percutants du Bauhaus, de l'architecture puriste de Le Corbusier aux sculptures énergiques d'Epstein et Gill. Cette période fut également propice aux monuments, dédiés au passé et aux morts pour la patrie, au futur avec des gratte-ciel et des barrages hydroélectriques et au présent avec des salles de cinéma géantes et des fabriques gigantesques.

The opening day of the British Empire Fair, White City, London, 20 February 1928. Two models show off their gaiters, 'fast becoming part of ladies' everyday wear'.

Eröffnungstag der Messe des Britischen Weltreichs, White City, London, 20. Februar 1928. Zwei Mannequins führen Gamaschen vor, die „im Handumdrehen zu einem Teil der Alltagsbekleidung für Damen werden“

Inauguration de l'Exposition de l'Empire britannique à White City, Londres, le 20 février 1928. Deux mannequins portent des guêtres qui « n'allaient pas tarder à faire partie de la garde-robe de tous les jours ».

Palm Beach fashions, 1925. The hat, the wide sleeves and the pleated skirt are unmistakably Twenties – chic and coquettish.

Palm-Beach-Mode, 1925. Der Hut, die weitgeschnittenen Ärmel und der Faltenrock entsprechen unverkennbar dem eleganten und koketten Stil der zwanziger Jahre.

La mode de Palm Beach, 1925.
Le chapeau, les manches amples et la jupe à plis sont typiques des années vingt – style chic et provocant.

Joan Crawford models a new dress, 1929. By then she had abandoned her earlier names of Lucille le Sueur and Billie Cassin.

Joan Crawford führt ein neues Modellkleid vor, 1929. Zu dieser Zeit hatte sie bereits ihre früheren Künstlernamen Lucille le Sueur und Billie Cassin abgelegt.

Joan Crawford présente une nouvelle robe, 1929. Elle avait depuis longtemps abandonné ses anciens noms, Lucille le Sueur et Billie Cassin.

Mrs A G McCorquodale steps out for the Santa Claus Ball, December 1929. Later, she became better known as Barbara Cartland. The dress is as ostentatious as its wearer.

Mrs. A. G. McCorquodale, die als Romanschriftstellerin unter dem Namen Barbara Cartland bekannt werden sollte, auf dem Weg zum Weihnachtsball, Dezember 1929. Das Kleid war ebenso auffällig wie die Frau, die es trug.

Mme A. G. McCorquodale prête pour le Bal de Noël, décembre 1929. Elle deviendra plus connue par la suite sous le nom de Barbara Cartland. La robe, à l'image de celle qui la porte, est très prétentieuse.

A model poses in a camisole, 1927. Originally, such a garment would have been called an 'under-bodice'. Comedians preferred the term 'camiknickers'.

Ein Mannequin posiert in einem Kamisol, 1927. Ursprünglich nannte man ein solches Kleidungsstück „Unter-Mieder". Komiker bevorzugten den Ausdruck „Damenhemdhose".

Un mannequin pose en « camisole », 1927. Ce genre de vêtement fut d'abord appelé « cache-corset ». Les humoristes préféraient quant à eux le terme de « chemise-culotte ».

The Anglo-Irish ballerina, Ninette de Valois, 1928. She was then principal dancer at Covent Garden, having earlier toured with Diaghilev's Ballets Russes.

Die anglo-irische Tänzerin Ninette de Valois, 1928. Nachdem sie mit Sergej Diaghilews Ballets Russes auf Tournee gegangen war, wurde sie Primaballerina des Königlichen Balletts von Covent Garden.

La ballerine anglo-irlandaise, Ninette de Valois, 1928. Elle fut nommée danseuse étoile au Covent Garden, après avoir effectué une série de tournées avec les Ballets Russes de Diaghilev.

New York, 1927. American choreographer Martha Graham in the ballet, *Strike*. She had already pioneered her own style of modern dance.

New York, 1927. Die amerikanische Choreographin Martha Graham in ihrem Ballett *Strike*. Sie leistete Pionierarbeit mit ihrem eigenen modernen Tanzstil, des Modern Dance.

New York, 1927. La chorégraphe américaine Martha Graham dansant dans le ballet *Strike*. Elle avait déjà créé son propre style de danse moderne.

Two sets of twins. Mary and Margie Angus (left), otherwise known as 'the Dolly Sisters of the Movies', 1929. The Dodge Twins (right), 1927, were professional dancers. The monocles add a Twenties touch to their outfits.

Zweimal Zwillinge. Mary und Margie Angus (links), auch bekannt unter dem Namen „die Dolly-Schwestern des Films“, 1929. Die Dodge-Zwillinge (rechts) waren professionelle Tänzerinnen. Die Monokel verleihen ihrem Aussehen einen Hauch der zwanziger Jahre.

Deux fois deux jumelles. Mary et Margie Angus (à gauche), également appelées « les sœurs Dolly du cinéma », 1929. Les « Dodge Twins » (à droite) étaient danseuses professionnelles, 1927. Le monocle ajoutait une touche « années vingt » à leur tenue.

'Give me my old straw hat and a double-trucking down the avenue we'll go…' – extract from a lyric of *The Old Routine*. Men from Dunn and Company, hatters, parade with piles of boaters, 1925.

„Gib mir meinen alten Strohhut, und wir werden den Boulevard hinunterzieh'n …", heißt es in dem Musical *The Old Routine*. Angestellte des Hutmachers Dunn and Company bei einem Balanceakt mit Strohhüten vor dem Geschäft, 1925.

« Passe-moi mon chapeau de paille et allons nous balader, bras dessus bras dessous, le long de l'avenue… » extrait d'une chanson de *The Old Routine*. Des employés de Dunn and Company, chapeliers, portant des piles de canotiers, 1925.

1925. Young debutantes in Kensington, London, receive instruction in the correct and incorrect way to retrieve a dropped handkerchief. It may be that you don't know which is the correct way – it's on the left – but most debutantes would have expected someone else to pick it up for them.

1925. Londoner Debütantinnen erhalten in Kensington Unterricht in Etikette. Hier lernen sie, ein fallengelassenes Taschentuch wieder aufzuheben. Die beiden Mädchen links zeigen, wie es richtig geht. Die Mehrzahl der Debütantinnen erwartet aber wohl, daß dies ein anderer für sie tut.

1925. Des débutantes à Kensington, Londres, apprennent à ramasser un mouchoir tombé par terre. Le geste à accomplir en pareilles circonstances est celui de gauche mais, à n'en pas douter, la plupart des débutantes pouvaient espérer que quelqu'un ramasse le mouchoir à leur place.

"Dolcian" FITTING SHOES
OX CALF, WILLOW CALF AND PATENT
FIVE 21/- FITTINGS

The window of a Dolcis shoe shop, November 1928. Heels tended to grow higher throughout the Twenties, and, for those who could afford new shoes, the variety available was intimidating.

Das Schaufenster eines Dolcis-Schuhgeschäfts, November 1928. Die Absätze wurden im Laufe der zwanziger Jahre immer höher, und für diejenigen, die sich neue Schuhe leisten konnten, war die Auswahl geradezu überwältigend.

Vitrine d'un magasin de chaussures Dolcis, novembre 1928. Dans les années vingt, la tendance était au talon toujours plus haut et, pour celles qui pouvaient s'offrir une nouvelle paire, le choix proposé était vertigineux.

Leg puller. Two models advertise new ladder-free stockings, Britain, 1926. The slogan on their cloaks proclaims the miraculously durable nature of a product which vanished long ago.

Blickfang. Zwei Mannequins werben für laufmaschensichere Strümpfe, Großbritannien, 1926. Der Werbespruch auf ihren Umhängen verkündet die wundersame Widerstandsfähigkeit eines Produktes, das mittlerweile niemand mehr kennt.

Attrape-nigauds. Ces deux mannequins font de la réclame pour des bas qui ne filent pas, Angleterre, 1926. Le slogan imprimé sur leurs capes affirme qu'ils durent miraculeusement longtemps. Ce produit n'existe plus.

The last word in smartness. A pair of black, lizard-trimmed shoes, 1925. The shoes could perhaps have come from some other decade, but the stockings are very Twenties.

Der letzte Schrei an Eleganz. Ein Paar mit Eidechsenleder verzierte Schuhe, 1925. Diese Schuhe hätte man vielleicht auch in einem anderen Jahrzehnt finden können, doch den Strümpfen sieht man an, daß sie aus den zwanziger Jahren stammen.

Le comble du chic. Une paire de chaussures noires bordées de peau de lézard, 1925. Les chaussures pourraient bien dater d'une autre époque, mais pas les bas, qui sont très « années vingt ».

Four young men smoking together outside their tent, 1922.
The headgear and the patterned shirts are perhaps too colourful to be considered fashionable, but smoking was definitely 'in' throughout the Twenties.

Vier junge Männer bei einer Zigarettenpause vor ihrem Zelt, 1922. Die Kopfbedeckungen und die stark gemusterten Hemden sind möglicherweise zu bunt, um als modisch zu gelten, doch das Rauchen war definitiv „in" in diesem Jahrzehnt.

Jeunes hommes fumant devant leur tente, 1922. Les bérets et le motif des chemises sont probablement trop colorés pour la mode de l'époque; par contre, fumer était très en vogue dans les années vingt.

May 1927. Bathing belles on the beach at Aldeburgh, Suffolk, on the east coast of Britain. It was a little early in the season to enjoy a North Sea beach – maybe they're smoking to keep warm.

Mai 1927. Badeschönheiten am Strand von Aldeburgh, Suffolk, an der Ostküste Englands. Es war noch zu früh in der Jahreszeit, um den Nordseestrand wirklich zu genießen – vielleicht rauchen sie Zigaretten, um sich warmzuhalten.

Mai 1927. Baigneuses sur la plage d'Aldeburgh, Suffolk, côte est de l'Angleterre. Il était encore un peu tôt dans la saison pour profiter d'une plage située au bord de la mer du Nord – fumer était peut-être une façon de se réchauffer.

Females on the catwalk. Models at the Artificial Silk Exhibition, Olympia, London, 1929. Not surprisingly, the outfits are all made from artificial silk.

Damen auf dem Laufsteg. Mannequins während einer Ausstellung von Kunstseide, Olympia, London, 1929. Selbstverständlich sind alle Modelle aus Kunstseide hergestellt.

Femmes sur le podium. Mannequins à l'Exposition de la soie artificielle, Olympia, Londres, 1929. Tous les modèles sont, bien entendu, réalisés en soie artificielle.

Males on the catwalk. A display of outdoor clothes at the Nottingham Cooperative Society showrooms, 1929. The caps and plus-fours (left) are very much in fashion, while the two little boys (right) could be mistaken for the heroes of any children's adventure story.

Herren auf dem Laufsteg. Eine Präsentation von Straßenkleidung in den Ausstellungsräumen der Genossenschaft von Nottingham, 1929. Die Mützen und Knickerbockerhosen der Herren (links) sind hochmodisch. Die beiden Jungen (rechts) könnte man leicht mit den Protagonisten in Lausbubengeschichten verwechseln.

Hommes sur le podium. Diverses tenues de sortie présentées au Salon de la Coopérative de Nottingham, 1929. Les casquettes et pantalons de golf (à gauche) sont très à la mode. Les deux garçons (à droite) ressemblent aux héros des livres d'aventures pour enfants de l'époque.

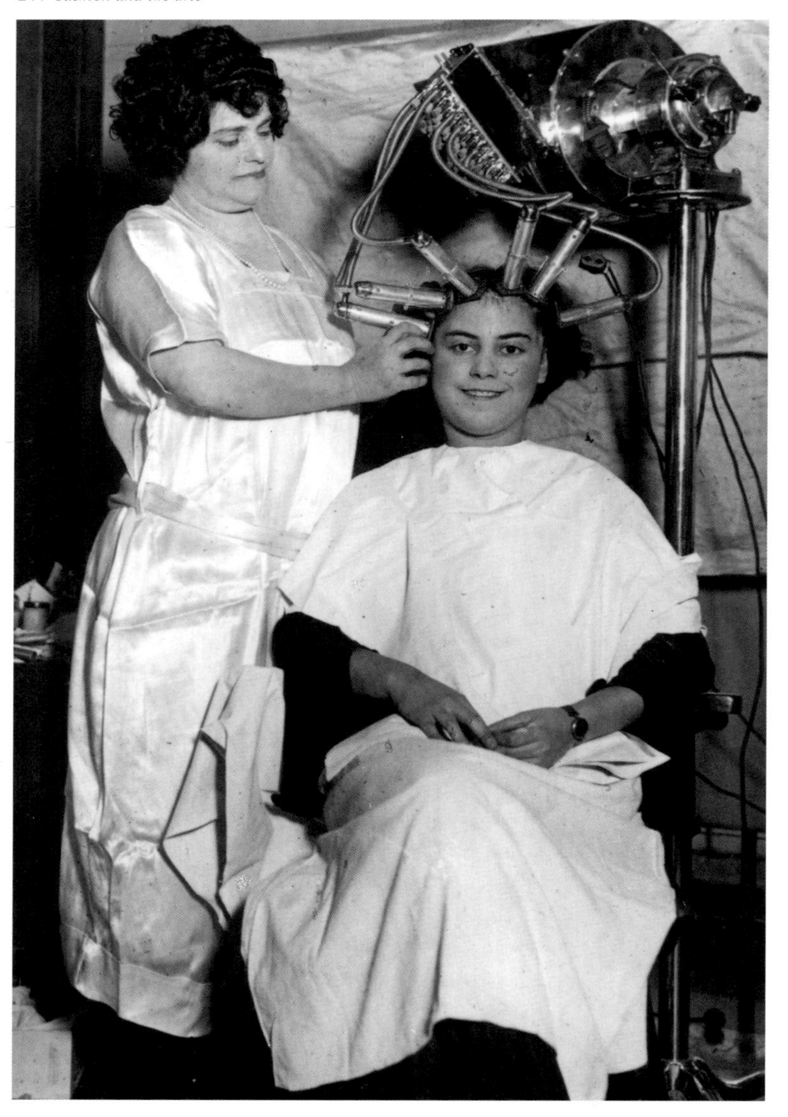

A new way to get a permanent wave, 1922. The process is American, the hair stylist is formidable, the grin is as permanent as the wave.

Eine neue Art von Dauerwelle, 1922. Das Verfahren stammt aus Amerika, die Friseuse wirkt bedrohlich, und das Grinsen ist vermutlich ebenso von Dauer wie die Welle.

Nouvelle méthode pour permanentes, 1922. Le procédé est américain, la coiffeuse formidable et le sourire aussi fixe que la future permanente.

Three members of the cast of *On With The Dance* proudly display their perms, 1921. The show was written by Noel Coward and produced by C B Cochran at the London Palladium. The hit number from the show was *Poor Little Rich Girl*.

Drei Mitwirkende des Musicals *On with the Dance* zeigen stolz ihre Frisuren, 1921. C. B. Cochran produzierte diese Show für das Londoner Palladium nach dem Buch von Noel Coward. Die erfolgreichste Nummer war *Armes, kleines, reiches Mädchen*.

Trois comédiennes de la comédie *On With The Dance* arborent fièrement leurs mis en plis, 1921. Le spectacle, écrit par Noel Coward et produit par C. B. Cochran, était joué au Palladium de Londres. La chanson la plus connue s'intitulait *Pauvre petite fille riche*.

Slimming in the Twenties, 1928. The machine is the Vibro-Slim, and its comic potential is enormous. The photographer was Henry Guttmann.

Abnehmen im Stil der zwanziger Jahre, 1928. Das Gerät Vibro-Slim, das Henry Guttmann fotografierte, besaß ein ungeheuer komisches Potential.

Maigrir dans les années vingt, 1928. Cet appareil est un Vibro-Slim et son utilisation comprend de nombreuses poses comiques, dont celle-ci, photographiée par Henry Guttmann.

A lady in a smoking suit, November 1922. For women to smoke in public was no longer considered 'fast' or daring, but few bothered to follow the male practice of wearing special clothes while smoking.

Eine Dame im Raucherkostüm, November 1922. Frauen, die in der Öffentlichkeit rauchten, galten damals nicht mehr als unanständig oder provozierend. Doch nur wenige von ihnen folgten der Praxis der Herren, beim Rauchen besondere Kleidung zu tragen.

Femme en habit de fumeur, novembre 1922. Il n'était plus mal vu ou osé pour une femme de fumer en public mais rares étaient celles qui, à l'instar des hommes, portaient des vêtements spécialement conçus pour cela.

Pedalling across the oceans – two women in the gym of the White Star Company's liner *Homeric*, February 1922. The liner had originally belonged to a German company, but was handed to Britain as part of the war reparations.

Mit dem Fahrrad über die Weltmeere – zwei Damen im Fitneßraum des Liniendampfers *Homeric* der White Star Company, Februar 1922. Das Schiff hatte ursprünglich einer deutschen Gesellschaft gehört, wurde aber Großbritannien als Teil der Kriegsreparationen übergeben.

Pédaler sur l'océan – deux femmes dans le gymnase du *Homeric* de la White Star Company, février 1922. Le paquebot avait appartenu à une compagnie allemande avant d'être cédé à la Grande-Bretagne pour réparations de guerre.

Galloping across the floor – two women ride a mechanical horse, 1925. Horse-riding, artificial or otherwise, was said to be good for the liver.

Auf dem Pferd durchs Zimmer – zwei Damen auf einem mechanischen Pferd, 1925. Zu jener Zeit war man der Meinung, daß Reiten in jedweder Form gut für die Leber sei.

Galoper en salle – deux femmes sur un cheval mécanique, 1925. L'équitation, que ce soit sur un vrai cheval ou non, était considérée comme un bon exercice pour le foie.

May 1929. Jacob Epstein at work on the figure of *Night* at the London Transport headquarters, St James's Park Station.

Mai 1929. Jacob Epstein bei der Arbeit an seiner Skulptur *Nacht*, die im Londoner Hauptverkehrsamt an der Station St. James's Park steht.

Mai 1929. Jacob Epstein à l'œuvre sur la sculpture *Nuit* destinée au siège de la Compagnie des transports de Londres, située à la gare de St. James' Park.

(From left to right) Lydia Sokolova, Anton Dolin, Bronislava Nijinska and Leon Woizikowsky in the Diaghilev Ballets Russes production of *Le Train Bleu*, London, 1924.

(Von links nach rechts) Lydia Sokolowa, Anton Dolin, Bronislawa Nijinska und Leon Wójcikowski in Diaghilews *Le Train Bleu* für die Tänzer des Ballets Russes, London 1924.

(De gauche à droite) Lydia Sokolova, Anton Dolin, Bronislava Nijinska et Leon Woizikowsky, danseurs des Ballets Russes de Diaghilev, à Londres, pour le spectacle intitulé *Le Train bleu*, 1924.

May 1928. Countess Seafield assists Cecil Beaton as he paints a vast canvas. Beaton had already made his name as a photographer and held a one-man show of his paintings at the Cooling Gallery, London. His greater fame as a theatrical designer was yet to come.

Mai 1928. Gräfin Seafield hilft Cecil Beaton beim Bemalen einer riesigen Leinwand. Beaton hatte sich bereits als Fotograf einen Namen gemacht und zeigte seine Gemälde in einer Einzelausstellung in der Londoner Cooling Gallery. Sein großer Erfolg als Bühnen- und Kostümbildner stand noch bevor.

Mai 1928. La comtesse Seafield aide Cecil Beaton à peindre cette grande toile. Beaton s'était déjà fait un nom comme photographe et exposait une série de tableaux à la Cooling Gallery de Londres. Par la suite, il deviendrait encore plus célèbre comme décorateur de théâtre.

Serge Lifar and Lubov Tchernicheva in *Le Pas d'Acier* at His Majesty's Theatre, London, July 1927.
The choreography was by Massine, the design by Yuri Yakoulov.

Serge Lifar und Lubow Tschernitschewa in *Le Pas d'Acier* im Londoner His Majesty's Theatre, Juli 1927. Die Choreographie stammte von Massine, die Ausstattung von Juri Jakulow.

Serge Lifar et Lubov Tchernicheva dans *Le Pas d'Acier* au His Majesty's Theatre de Londres, juillet 1927. La chorégraphie était signée Massine et le décor était de Yuri Yakoulov.

The world-famous Russian ballerina Anna Pavlova, in costume for the ballet *Assyrian Dance*, 1921.

Die weltberühmte russische Ballerina Anna Pawlowa im Kostüm für das Ballett *Assyrian Dance*, 1921.

Anna Pavlova, ballerine russe mondialement célèbre, en habit de scène pour le ballet *Danse assyrienne*, 1921.

1928. The Art Deco stairway in the hall of Dorville House, Cavendish Square, London. Dorville House was the headquarters of Rose and Blairman.

1928. Das Treppenhaus im Art-Déco-Stil im Dorville House am Londoner Cavendish Square. Diese Villa war der Hauptsitz von Rose and Blairman.

1928. L'escalier Art Déco de l'entrée de la Dorville House, située à Cavendish Square, Londres. Cette demeure était le siège de la maison Rose et Blairman.

Classic interiors of the Twenties. The futuristic Catholic church at Ulm, Germany, September 1928.

Innenarchitektur im Stil der zwanziger Jahre. Die futuristisch anmutende katholische Kirche in Ulm, September 1928.

Intérieur typique des années vingt. L'église catholique de style futuriste à Ulm, Allemagne, septembre 1928.

Inside the Strand Palace Hotel, London, 1925. The original entrance is now in the Victoria and Albert Museum.

Im Londoner Strand Palace Hotel, 1925. Diese Eingangshalle befindet sich heute im Victoria and Albert Museum.

L'entrée du Strand Palace Hotel à Londres, 1925. Le décor d'origine est aujourd'hui exposé au Victoria and Albert Museum, Londres.

7. Science
Wissenschaft
La Science

Technicians put the finishing touches to a giant model camera from the Ernamen works before the start of a photography exhibition in Berlin, 1927.

Zwei Techniker legen vor Beginn einer Berliner Fotografie-Ausstellung letzte Hand an ein überdimensionales Kameramodell der Ernamen-Werke, 1927.

Des techniciens procèdent aux derniers réglages de cet appareil géant, fabriqué par Ernamen, avant l'ouverture d'une exposition de photographie à Berlin, 1927.

"ERNOSTAR"
D.R.P
DEN · ERNE
ERNEM

7. Science
Wissenschaft
La Science

There are some that say the greatest discovery of the Twenties was that Prohibition didn't work, but it was a decade rich in the fruits of science and exploration. By the time the phonograph celebrated its 50th anniversary in 1927, the art of recording sound had reached new levels of sophistication, though reproduction was still comparatively primitive. Within a year or two television had been born, you could phone direct from London to San Francisco, and the arrival of the 'talkies' had panicked Hollywood.

In successive years Albert Einstein and Niels Bohr were Nobel prize-winners for their work on the quantum theory, and in 1924 Willem Einthoven won the Nobel prize for Physiology and Medicine after he pioneered the electrocardiogram. Four years later Alexander Fleming discovered penicillin. Modern medicine in many ways dates from the Twenties.

The most famous discovery of the age was that of Tutankhamen's tomb by Howard Carter and Lord Carnarvon in November 1922. The riches they found there – and maybe plundered – captured the world's imagination, and for a while 'Tut Fever' raged. Carnarvon hardly survived long enough to realize how famous he had become – he died six months later of blood poisoning from an insect bite he had suffered while excavating the tomb.

Böse Zungen behaupten, die größte Entdeckung der zwanziger Jahre sei die Erkenntnis gewesen, daß die Prohibition ein Fehlschlag war. Doch in diesem Jahrzehnt gelangen auch wirklich wichtige Erfindungen. Als der Phonograph 1927 seinen 50. Geburtstag feierte, hatte die Aufnahmetechnik entscheidende Verfeinerungen erfahren. Die Wiedergabe steckte im Vergleich dazu allerdings noch immer in den Kinderschuhen. Ein bis zwei Jahre nach der Erfindung des Fernsehens konnte man bereits von London nach San Francisco telefonieren, und die Entwicklung des Tonfilms hatte Hollywood in helle Aufregung versetzt.

In aufeinanderfolgenden Jahren gewannen Albert Einstein und Niels Bohr den Nobelpreis für Physik. Beide Wissenschaftler hatten sich mit der Quantentheorie beschäftigt. Der Niederländer Willem Einthoven erhielt 1924 den Nobelpreis für Physiologie und Medizin. Er leistete Pionierarbeit in der Elektrokardiographie. Vier Jahre später entdeckte Alexander Fleming das Penicillin. In vielerlei Hinsicht wurzelt die moderne Medizin in der Forschung der zwanziger Jahre.

Die berühmteste Entdeckung des Jahrzehnts gelang im November 1922. Howard Carter und Lord Carnarvon entdeckten die Grabstätte Tutenchamuns. Die Schätze, die sie in der Gruft vorfanden – und vielleicht auch plünderten – beflügelten die Phantasie der Menschen. Eine Zeitlang herrschte ein regelrechtes „Tutenchamun-Fieber". Carnarvon konnte seinen Ruhm aber nicht genießen, da er bereits sechs Monate nach der Graböffnung an einer Blutvergiftung starb, die er sich bei den Ausgrabungen durch einen Insektenstich zugezogen hatte.

Pour certains, la plus grande découverte des années vingt fut la preuve que la prohibition ne servit à rien, mais cette affirmation ne saurait cacher les progrès de la science et les découvertes réalisées au cours de cette décennie. En 1927, alors que l'on fêtait les 50 ans du phonographe, les techniques d'enregistrement étaient plus sophistiquées que jamais, même si la reproduction était encore très élémentaire. Un ou deux ans après que, la télévision fit son apparition. A Londres, il était possible d'appeler San Francisco sans passer par une opératrice et à Hollywood, l'avènement des films parlants semait la panique.

Albert Einstein et Niels Bohr obtinrent successivement le prix Nobel pour leur travail sur la théorie quantique et, en 1924, Willem Einthoven reçut le prix Nobel de la physiologie et de la médecine pour ses recherches sur l'électrocardiogramme. Quatre ans plus tard, Alexander Fleming découvrait la pénicilline. La médecine moderne doit beaucoup aux années vingt.

La plus célèbre découverte de la décennie fut celle de la tombe de Toutankhamon par Howard Carter et Lord Carnarvon, en novembre 1922. Les richesses qu'ils y trouvèrent – et peut-être pillèrent – captivèrent le monde entier et pendant quelque temps la « fièvre du Toutankhamon » fit rage. Carnarvon ne vécut pas assez longtemps pour réaliser à quel point il était devenu célèbre. Il mourut six mois plus tard des suites d'une piqûre d'insecte survenue pendant l'excavation de la tombe qui lui provoqua un empoisonnement du sang.

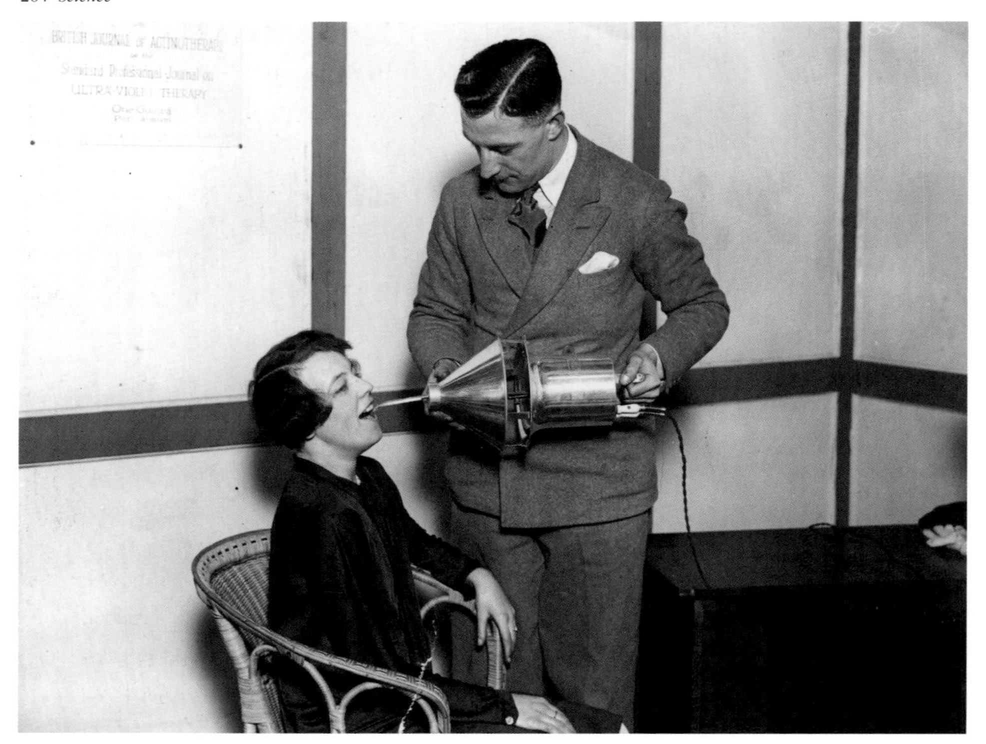

1927. The Sunviray dental lamp being demonstrated at the first International Exhibition of Light and Heat in Medicine, Westminster, London. It was the great age of rays – death rays, health rays, rays of destruction and rays that healed.

1927. Auf der ersten Internationalen Ausstellung für Licht und Wärme in der Medizin wird im Londoner Stadtteil Westminster die zahnmedizinische Lampe von Sunviray vorgeführt. Das Zeitalter der Strahlentechnik war angebrochen – man erforschte die Wirkung von tödlichen und gesunden, von zerstörenden und heilenden Strahlen.

1927. Démonstration de la lampe dentaire de Sunviray lors de la première Exposition internationale de l'équipement médical utilisant la lumière et la chaleur, Westminster, Londres. Ce fut la grande époque des rayons de toutes sortes, allant des rayons mortels aux rayons à usage médical.

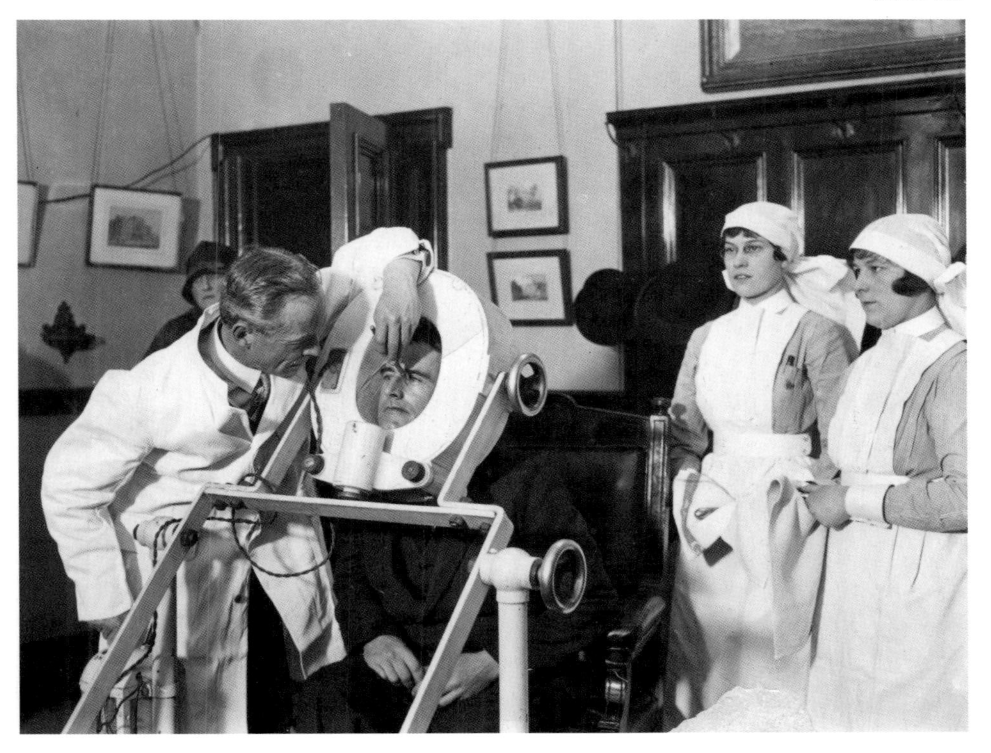

Britain, 1927. A patient is examined for steel splinters. Many jobs in the burgeoning light industries involved the use of lathes or stamps that produced tiny splinters of metal. This machine was supposed to locate and remove them.

Großbritannien, 1927. Das Gesicht eines Patienten wird auf Stahlsplitter untersucht. In der expandierenden Leichtindustrie gab es viele Dreh- oder Stanzarbeiten zu verrichten, bei denen winzige Metallsplitter flogen. Das abgebildete Gerät sollte diese lokalisieren und entfernen.

Grande-Bretagne, 1927. Ce patient a reçu des éclats de métal. De nombreux emplois créés dans l'industrie légère naissante nécessitaient la manipulation de lames et de poinçons provoquant des éclats de métal. Cet appareil était censé les localiser et les extraire.

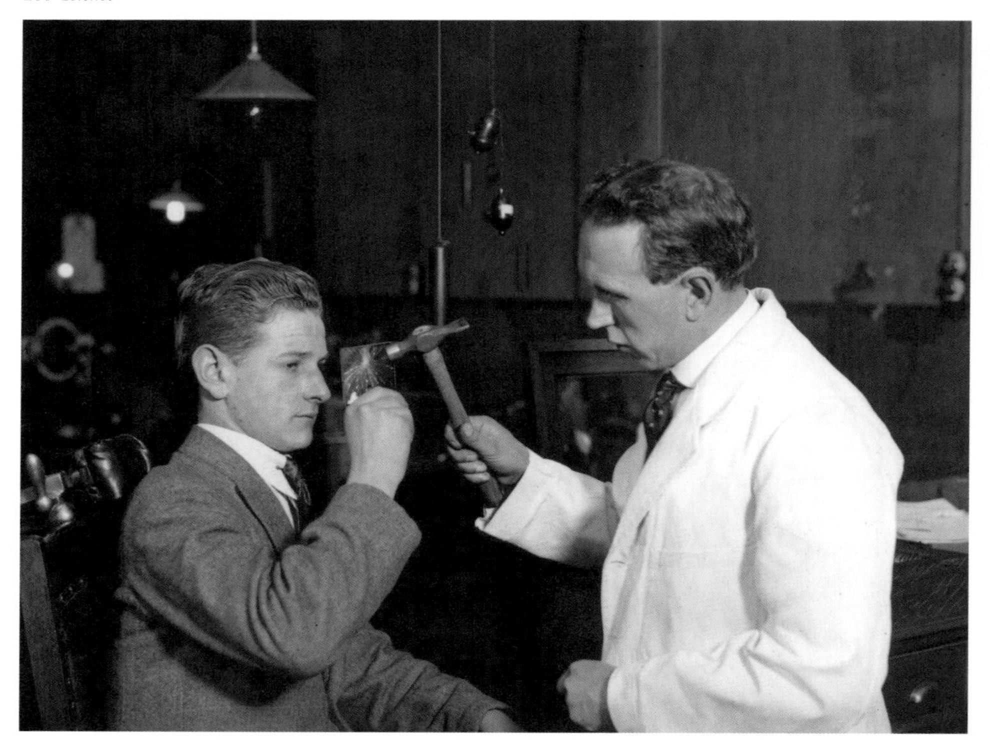

A telling demonstration of the qualities of Triplex Safety Glass, 1925. Originally it was manufactured for use in spectacles, where its non-splintering properties would save damage to the eyes. Later it was widely used in car windscreens.

Eine eindrucksvolle Demonstration der Qualität von Triplex-Sicherheitsglas, 1925. Ursprünglich war es als Brillenglas entwickelt worden, da seine splittersicheren Eigenschaften das Auge vor Verletzungen schützten. Später kam es bei Autowindschutzscheiben zum Einsatz.

Une démonstration parlante de la résistance du verre de sécurité Triplex, 1925. Inventé à l'origine pour les lunettes parce qu'il ne faisait pas d'èclats en se brisant et ne risquait pas de blesser l'œil, il fut ensuite beaucoup utilisé pour les pare-brise de voiture.

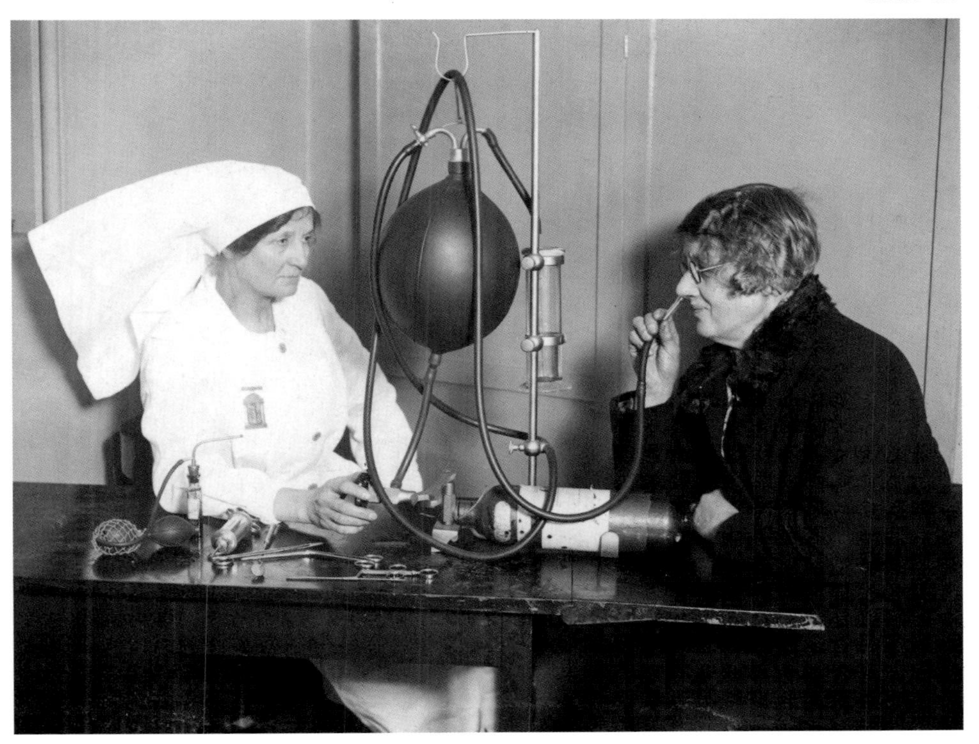

A machine for the relief of asthma, 1929. In the age of coal fires and massive industrial smoke pollution, asthma sufferers led miserable lives.

Ein Gerät, das Asthma-Kranken Erleichterung verschaffen sollte, 1929. Im Zeitalter der Kohleöfen und der massiven industriellen Luftverschmutzung hatten es besonders die Asthmatiker schwer.

Appareil destiné à soulager les asthmatiques, 1929. A une époque où l'on brûlait du charbon dans les cheminées et où la pollution industrielle était très élevée, les asthmatiques avaient la vie dure.

The top deck of a bus is sprayed with an anti-influenza compound during the epidemic of 1920. More people in Europe died of influenza at this time than had been killed in World War I.

Während der Grippe-Epidemie von 1920 wird das Oberdeck eines Busses mit einem Grippeschutzmittel ausgesprüht. Während dieser Epidemie starben in Europa mehr Menschen als im Ersten Weltkrieg.

La plate-forme de ce bus est désinfectée avec un produit anti-grippe durant l'épidémie de 1920. En Europe, cette épidémie de grippe fit plus de victimes que la Première Guerre mondiale.

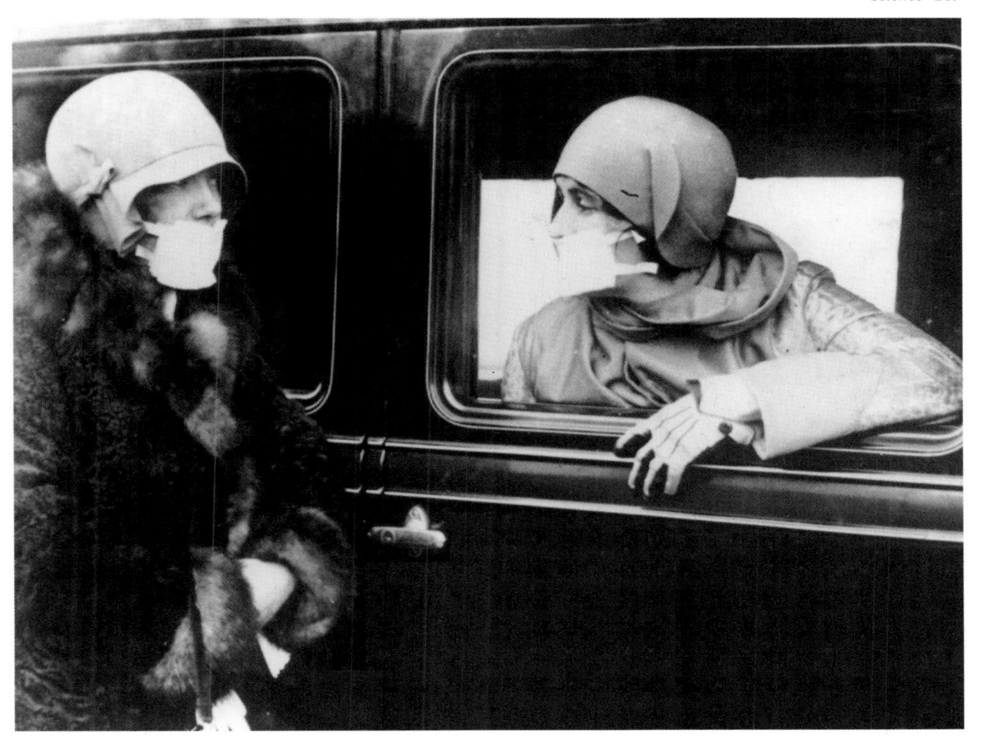

Other means of protection – two women wear masks during the same epidemic. The disease was not confined to Europe. It spread to the United States and Asia.

Weitere Schutzmaßnahmen – zwei Frauen tragen einen Mundschutz während der Epidemie. Die Grippewelle breitete sich über die Grenzen Europas aus, sogar bis in die Vereinigten Staaten und nach Asien.

Autres moyens de protection – deux femmes portent un masque durant la même épidémie. La maladie ne se limita pas à l'Europe, mais se répandit également aux Etats-Unis et en Asie.

'Tut Fever', 1922. Dolores Denis Denison arrives at a fashionable party dressed as an Egyptian mummy. News of the discovery of Tutankhamen's tomb by Carter and Carnarvon travelled quickly.

„Tutenchamun-Fieber", 1922. Dolores Denis Denison erscheint auf einer vornehmen Gesellschaft im Kostüm einer ägyptischen Mumie. Die Nachricht von der Entdeckung der Grabstätte Tutenchamuns durch die Engländer Carter und Carnarvon verbreitete sich schnell.

La « fièvre du Toutankhamon », 1922. Dolores Denis Denison se rend à un bal costumé dans un lieu à la mode, déguisée en momie égyptienne. La nouvelle de la découverte de la tombe de Toutankhamon par Carter et Carnarvon s'était vite répandue.

Howard Carter, kneeling, unseals the entrance to the fourth chamber of Tutankhamen's tomb, Egypt, 1923.

Howard Carter, knieend, öffnet den versiegelten Eingang zur vierten Kammer der Grabstätte Tutenchamuns, Ägypten, 1923.

Howard Carter, à genoux, défait le sceau de la quatrième chambre de la tombe de Toutankhamon, Egypte, 1923.

Decorators at work in the Egyptian Gallery at the Crystal Palace, South London, 1926. With its long avenues of lions, mummies and sphinxes, it was the most impressive court in the entire exhibition, even though much of it had been gutted by fire in 1867.

Dekorateurinnen bei der Arbeit in der ägyptischen Galerie des Süd-Londoner Crytal Palace, 1926. Mit ihren imposanten, von Löwen, Mumien und Sphingen gesäumten Wandelgängen war dies die eindrucksvollste Halle der gesamten Ausstellung, die in der Feuersbrunst von 1867 größtenteils ausgebrannt war.

Décorateurs à l'œuvre dans la galerie de l'Egypte du Crystal Palace, sud de Londres, 1926. Avec ses grandes rangées de lions, de momies et de sphinx, cette salle était la plus spectaculaire de toute l'exposition, malgré la perte de nombreuses pièces, détruites dans l'incendie de 1867.

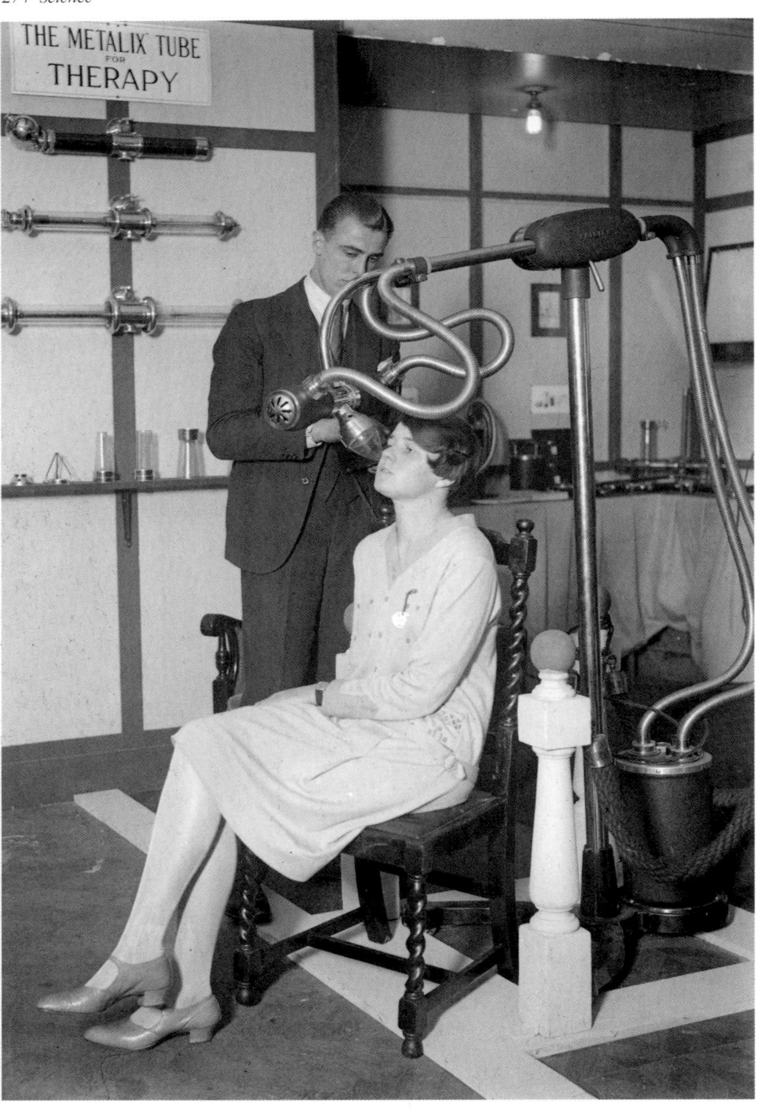

Therapy, 1928 style. The machine, on display at an X-ray Exhibition in London, was called 'The Metalix Tube for Therapy'.

Therapie im Stil der zwanziger Jahre, 1928. Der „Metalix-Therapieschlauch" war auf einer Ausstellung über Röntgenstrahlen in London zu sehen.

Thérapie de l'époque, 1928. Cet appareil, présenté dans le cadre d'une exposition sur les rayons X, s'appelait « le tube thérapeutique de Métalix ».

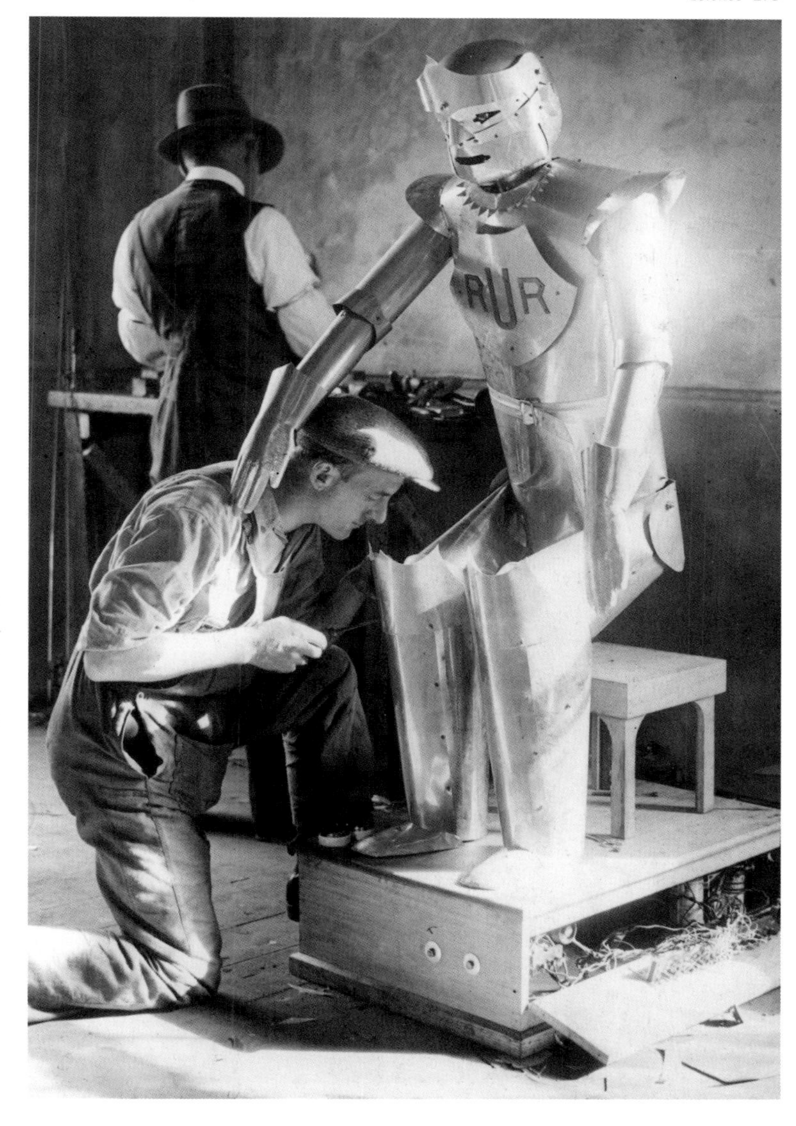

Making adjustments to Captain Richards' robot, August 1928. The robot could speak, shake hands, tell the time and sit down. Productivity was not its strong point.

Hauptmann Richards' Roboter benötigt eine letzte Korrektur seiner Einstellungen, August 1928. Er konnte sprechen, zur Begrüßung die Hand reichen, die Uhrzeit mitteilen und sich hinsetzen. Produktivität war nicht gerade einer seiner Stärken.

Derniers réglages sur le robot du capitaine Richards, août 1928. Ce robot pouvait parler, serrer la main, donner l'heure et s'asseoir. La productivité n'était pas son fort.

Members of a mine rescue team practise moving in their protective clothing at Wheatley colliery, Doncaster, Yorkshire, 1925. Mine disasters were frequent and horrendous in the Twenties.

Mitarbeiter einer Rettungsmannschaft lernen in der Wheatley-Zeche in Doncaster, Yorkshire, sich in ihrer neuen Schutzkleidung zu bewegen, 1925. Die häufigen Grubenunglücke der zwanziger Jahren hatten meist verheerende Folgen.

L'un des membres de l'équipe de secours fait un essai, vêtu d'une combinaison de protection, à la mine de Wheatley, Yorkshire, 1925. Dans les années vingt, les accidents dans les mines étaient fréquents et dramatiques.

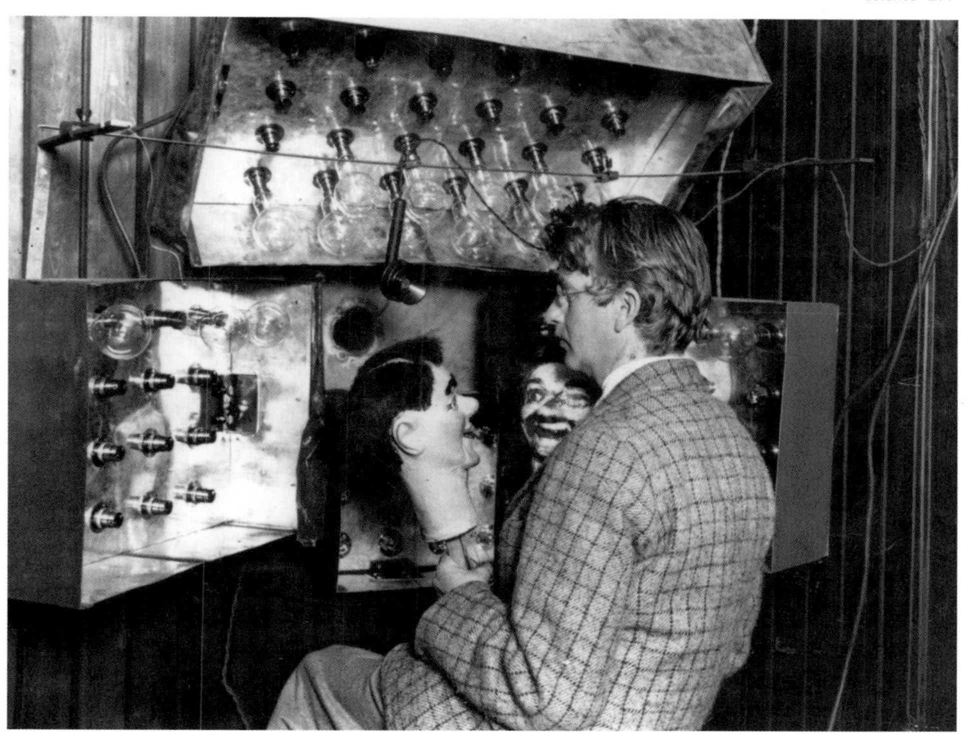

1926. John Logie Baird demonstrates his new invention with the aid of two ventriloquist's dummies. Development of television was staggeringly swift. By 1928, General Electric were broadcasting plays on radio and television simultaneously. A year later, the Bell Company pioneered colour TV.

1926. John Logie Baird stellt seine neue Erfindung mit Hilfe zweier Bauchrednerpuppen vor. Die Entwicklung des Fernsehens vollzog sich in ungeheurer Geschwindigkeit. 1928 gelang der Gesellschaft General Electric die Simultanübertragung von Theaterstücken im Radio und Fernsehen. Bereits ein Jahr später brachte die Bell Company Farbfernseher auf den Markt.

1926. John Logie Baird présente sa dernière invention, aidé de deux poupées de ventriloque. La télévision évoluait étonnamment vite. En 1928 déjà, General Electric diffusait des pièces de théâtre simultanément à la radio et à la télévision. Un an plus tard, la Bell Company lançait la télévision couleur.

8. Transport
Transportwesen
Les moyens de transport

October 1928. The *Graf Zeppelin* flies over the Brandenburg Gate, Berlin. The *Graf Zeppelin* was the flying wonder of the age. It crossed the Atlantic, flew round the world, and carried passengers, airmail, a consignment of canaries, a gorilla and a grand piano.

Oktober 1928. Der *Graf Zeppelin,* schwebt über das Brandenburger Tor in Berlin. Das Luftschiff galt als fliegendes Wunder dieser Zeit. Es überquerte den Atlantik, umflog die ganze Welt und beförderte nicht nur Passagiere und Luftpost, sondern auch Kanarienvögel, einen Gorilla und einen Konzertflügel.

Octobre 1928. Le *Graf Zeppelin* au-dessus de la porte de Brandebourg, Berlin. Ce zeppelin était le miracle volant de l'époque. Il traversa l'Atlantique et fit le tour du monde avec, à son bord, des passagers, du courir postal, des canaris, un gorille et même un piano à queue.

8. Transport
Transportwesen
Les moyens de transport

Trains, planes, airships, ocean liners, fast cars – the Twenties had them all – and though some of the designs may now seem comically old-fashioned, there was also a great deal of style in the monsters that sailed the oceans, climbed the clouds, or steamed along the railway lines.

On the roads, the Chryslers, de Dions, Franklin sports coupés, and Dusenbergs that purred down Main Street had a grace that has never been recaptured. On the racetracks, the Mercedes, Bugattis, and Maseratis that gathered on the grid at Brooklands, Le Mans or on the Avus Circuit at Grunewald were among the most beautiful racing cars ever seen. In 1927 Major H O D Seagrave became the first man to travel at over 200 mph (320 kph) in a car.

Two months later, Charles Lindbergh had landed *The Spirit of St Louis* in Paris after completing the first solo flight across the Atlantic. There were far more comfortable ways of crossing the Atlantic. The passenger liners of the Twenties were floating five-star hotels – elegant, lavishly furnished, with a standard of service that rivalled anything the Waldorf Astoria, the Ritz or the Savoy could offer.

For those with humbler tastes and thinner wallets, Henry Ford supplied his 15 millionth 'Tin Lizzie' in May 1927. And if that was too expensive, there was always the tram.

Eisenbahnen, Flugzeuge, Luftschiffe, Ozeandampfer und schnelle Autos – all das gab es bereits in den zwanziger Jahren. Und wenn auch einige der Modelle aus heutiger Sicht hoffnungslos altmodisch wirken mögen, besaßen diese Monster, die die Ozeane überquerten, sich in die Lüfte erhoben oder über Eisenbahnschienen ratterten, sehr viel Stil und Eleganz.

Chryslers, de Dions, Franklin-Sportwagen und Dusenbergs bewegten sich mit einer Anmut über die Straßen, die später nie wieder erreicht wurde. Auf den Rennstrecken in Brooklands, Le Mans oder dem Avus-Ring im Grunewald versammelten sich die schönsten Rennwagen von

Mercedes, Bugatti und Maserati, die es je gab. Im Jahre 1927 erreichte Major H. O. D. Seagrave erstmals eine Geschwindigkeit von 320 km/h mit einem Auto.

Zwei Monate später landete Charles Lindbergh nach erfolgreicher Erstüberquerung des Atlantischen Ozeans im Alleingang sein Flugzeug *The Spirit of St. Louis* in Paris. Es gab allerdings eine sehr viel bequemere Art, den Großen Teich zu überqueren, denn die Passagierschiffe der zwanziger Jahre glichen schwimmenden Fünf-Sterne-Hotels. Sie waren elegant und luxuriös ausgestattet und boten einen hervorragenden Service, der es ohne weiteres mit dem Waldorf Astoria, dem Ritz oder dem Savoy aufnehmen konnte.

Für diejenigen, die einen einfacheren Geschmack und einen schmaleren Geldbeutel hatten, ließ Henry Ford im Mai 1927 die 15millionste „Tin Lizzie" vom Band rollen. Und wem auch das noch zu kostspielig war, der konnte mit der Straßenbahn fahren.

Les années vingt ont tout connu : les trains, les avions, les dirigeables, les transatlantiques et les voitures de course. Même si le style de l'époque peut nous paraître aujourd'hui comique et désuet, il n'en reste pas moins que ces monstres qui franchissaient les océans, s'élevaient dans les airs ou sifflaient à toute vapeur le long des voies ferrées avaient grande allure.

Sur les routes, les Chrysler, les de Dions, les coupés Franklin ou les Dusenberg descendant les grandes avenues, avaient une grâce restée inégalée. Sur les circuits de Brooklands, du Mans ou de Grunewald, les Mercedes, les Bugatti et les Maserati qui s'alignaient sur les grilles de départ figurent parmi les plus belles voitures de course jamais élaborées. En 1927, le commandant H. O. D. Seagrave fut le premier à conduire une voiture à plus de 320 km/heure.

Deux mois plus tard, Charles Lindbergh atterrissait à Paris à bord de son avion, *The Spirit of St. Louis*, après avoir effectué la première traversée de l'Atlantique en solitaire. Mais il y avait des façons bien plus confortables de traverser l'Atlantique. Les passagers des paquebots des années vingt voyageaient dans des hôtels cinq étoiles flottants – élégants, somptueusement meublés, offrant un service qui rivalisait avec le Waldorf Astoria, le Ritz ou le Savoy.

Pour ceux qui avaient des goûts plus simples et un portefeuille moins garni, Henry Ford fabriqua en mai 1927 sa 15 millionième voiture, la fameuse « Tin Lizzie ». Et, si c'était encore trop cher, il restait le tram.

November 1929. Four US airships anchored on the ground. The original airships were nicknamed 'flying gherkins', but by the end of the decade they had proved their worth. It was not until the disasters of the *R101* and the *Hindenburg* in the Thirties that the airship era came to an end.

November 1929. Vier am Boden verankerte, amerikanische Luftschiffe. Die ersten Luftschiffe erhielten den Spitznamen „fliegende Gewürzgurken", doch bis zum Ende des Jahrzehnts hatten sie ihren Wert unter Beweis gestellt. Erst als die *R101* und die *Hindenburg* in den dreißiger Jahren verunglückten, ging das große Zeitalter der Luftschiffe zu Ende.

Novembre 1929. Quatre dirigeables américains amarrés au sol. Les premiers modèles furent surnommés « cornichons volants », mais ils surent, avant la fin des années vingt, conquérir leurs lettres de noblesse. L'ère des dirigeables prit fin dans les années trente après la catastrophe du *R101* et du *Hindenburg*.

Giant and midget, May 1927. The *Flying Scotsman* towers over the *Typhoon* of the Romney, Hythe and Dymchurch narrow gauge railway. In 1928 the *Flying Scotsman* hauled the first non-stop rail service between London and Edinburgh, a distance of almost 400 miles (640 kilometres).

Ein Riese und ein Zwerg, Mai 1927. Die *Flying Scotsman* zeigt ihre wahre Größe neben dem kleinen *Typhoon* der Romney, Hythe und Dymchurch Schmalspureisenbahn. 1928 verkehrte die *Flying Scotsman* als erster Direktzug zwischen London und Edinburgh, eine Entfernung von annähernd 640 Kilometern.

Géant et minuscule, mai 1927. La *Flying Scotsman* domine la *Typhoon* de la société de chemin de 1er à voie étroite de Romney, Hythe et Dymchurch. En 1928, la *Flying Scotsman* effectua le premier parcours sans escale Londres-Edimbourg, soit près de 640 kilomètres.

Toys for the boys. J H Thomas, soon to be Lord Privy Seal in the British government, drives a miniature train round the estate of Sir Edward Nichol, July 1927.

Das Kind im Manne. J. H. Thomas, dem bald nach dieser Aufnahme das Amt des Lordsiegelbewahrers im britischen Kabinett übertragen wurde, steuert eine Miniatureisenbahn über das Anwesen von Sir Edward Nichol, Juli 1927.

Jouet pour garçons. J. H. Thomas, futur lord du sceau privé au sein du gouvernement britannique, fait circuler un train miniature à travers la propriété de Sir Edward Nichol, juillet 1927.

October 1928. German boys admire their toy Zeppelin. With a cruising speed of 62 mph (100 kph), the real thing was then as glamorous and exciting as a space rocket is to modern children.

Oktober 1928. Deutsche Jungen bewundern ihren Spielzeug-Zeppelin. Mit einer Reisegeschwindigkeit von 100 km/h war das reale Luftschiff für sie damals genauso faszinierend und aufregend wie eine moderne Weltraumrakete für die Kinder von heute.

Octobre 1928. Petits Allemands admirant leur zeppelin miniature. Avec une vitesse de croisière de 100 km/heure, le vrai dirigeable était à cette époque aussi incroyable et fascinant qu'une fusée peut l'être pour un enfant d'aujourd'hui.

The SS *Majestic* sits in dry dock, November 1922. The queens of the ocean in the Twenties were the *Aquitania* and *Mauretania* and the *Vaterland*, which was seized in New York harbour as part of war reparations and renamed the *Leviathan*.

Die SS *Majestic* im Trockendock, November 1922. In den zwanziger Jahren beherrschten drei Schiffe die Weltmeere: die *Aquitania*, die *Mauretania* und die *Vaterland*, die im Hafen von New York als Teil der Kriegsreparationen beschlagnahmt und in *Leviathan* umbenannt wurde.

Le SS *Majestic* en cale sèche, novembre 1922. Dans les années vingt, les rois de l'océan étaient l'*Aquitania*, le *Mauretania* et le *Vaterland*, saisi dans le port de New York à titre de réparations de guerre, puis rebaptisé *Leviathan*.

1925. The British airship *R33* is assembled, as the skeleton of the nose is manoeuvred into position.

1925. Das britische Luftschiff *R33* steht kurz vor der Fertigstellung, als der vordere Teil in Position gebracht wird.

1925. Assemblage du dirigeable britannique *R33* et mise en place du nez.

June 1928. The monoplane *Inflexible* waits on the tarmac at Croydon Airport. *Inflexible* was the biggest aeroplane in the world.

Juni 1928. Der Eindecker *Inflexible* wartet auf dem Rollfeld des Flughafens von Croydon. Die *Inflexible* war damals das größte Flugzeug der Welt.

Juin 1928. Le monoplan *Inflexible* sur la piste de l'aéroport de Croydon. L'*Inflexible* fut le plus grand avion jamais construit.

1928. The Beardmore-Rohrbach *Inflexible*, with a 140-foot (43-metre) wingspan. Probably the most impressive and useless plane of its age, it was nicknamed the *Impossible*.

1928. Die *Inflexible* von Beardmore und Rohrbach besaß eine Spannweite von 43 Metern. Wahrscheinlich das eindrucksvollste und nutzloseste Flugzeug seiner Zeit, erhielt es den Spitznamen *Impossible*.

1928. L'*Inflexible* de Beardmore-Rohrbach avait des ailes mesurant 43 mètres de long. Cet avion, probablement le plus massif et le plus inutile de toute l'histoire de l'aviation, fut surnommé l'*Impossible*.

In-flight service. A flight attendant serves drinks to passengers on a French airliner flying from Paris to London, April 1929. By the late Twenties there were regular scheduled flights between most European capitals.

Bordservice. Ein Flugbegleiter serviert Getränke in einem französischen Verkehrsflugzeug auf der Strecke Paris-London, April 1929. In den späten zwanziger Jahren gab es bereits regelmäßige Linienflugverbindungen zwischen den meisten europäischen Hauptstädten.

Service à bord. Un steward sert des boissons aux passagers du vol Paris-Londres, avril 1929. Il y avait, dès la fin des années vingt, des vols réguliers à destination de la plupart des capitales européennes.

In-flight movies. Passengers watch the first film ever shown on an airliner, 1925. The seats may have been less comfortable than modern ones, but the large windows gave far better views if the movie wasn't up to scratch.

Bordkino. Diese Fluggäste sehen den ersten Film, der in einem Verkehrsflugzeug gezeigt wurde, 1925. Die Sitze waren zwar nicht so bequem wie heute, doch die großen Fenster boten den Passagieren eine bessere Aussicht, falls der Film nicht den Erwartungen entsprach.

Cinéma à bord. Des passagers regardent le premier film projeté dans un avion, 1925. Les sièges n'étaient pas aussi confortables qu'aujourd'hui mais les fenêtres étaient plus grandes, offrant ainsi une meilleure vue au cas où le film manquait d'intérêt.

Night train, US style, September 1928. The interior of one of the cross-continental sleeping cars.

Ein Nachtzug im amerikanischen Stil, September 1928. Ein Schlafwagenabteil in einem Transkontinentalzug.

Train de nuit américain, septembre 1928. Intérieur d'une cabine en wagon-lit d'un train effectuant la traversée des Etats-Unis.

Night train, British style, September 1928. The interior of a third-class sleeping coach on the London and North Eastern Railway.

Ein Nachtzug im britischen Stil, September 1928. Ein Schlafwagenabteil dritter Klasse der Eisenbahngesellschaft LNER, London and North Eastern Railway.

Train de nuit britannique, septembre 1928. Intérieur d'un compartiment couchettes de 3e classe de la compagnie London and North Eastern Railway.

A battery of ticket machines at Piccadilly Tube Station, 1928. This was the year the station opened, attracting attention from all over the world. A delegation from Moscow was sent by Stalin to study the design and workings of the station.

Fahrkartenautomaten in der U-Bahn-Station Piccadilly, 1928. In jenem Jahr wurde diese U-Bahn-Haltestelle eröffnet, die weltweit Aufmerksamkeit erregte. Unter anderem schickte Stalin eine Moskauer Delegation, die die Konstruktion der Station und die Abfertigung der Fahrgäste studierte.

Distributeur de billets à la station de métro de Piccadilly, 1928. Ouverte cette année-là, la station suscita la curiosité du monde entier. Staline envoya une délégation de Moscou pour étudier la conception et le fonctionnement de la station.

Customer complaints, 1922. A passenger – probably disgruntled – records his comments on a blank poster provided for that purpose on the London Underground.

Reklamationen, 1922. Ein wohl verstimmter Fahrgast notiert seine Beschwerde auf einer hierfür vorgesehenen Tafel in der Londoner U-Bahn.

Réclamations, 1922. Un voyageur, probablement mécontent, dépose sa réclamation sur un panneau affiché à cet effet dans le métro de Londres.

A day at the races, 1921. A child is helped on to a charabanc which is about to set off for a race meeting somewhere in England. The charabanc, or motor coach, was the favourite vehicle for all outings.

Ein Tag auf der Pferderennbahn,1921. Ein Kind wird auf einen offenen Omnibus hinaufgereicht, der zu einem der zahlreichen englischen Pferderennen fährt. Der Charabanc war das beliebteste Transportmittel für Ausflugsfahrten.

Une journée aux courses, 1921. Un enfant est hissé à bord d'un autocar prêt à partir au champ de courses quelque part en Angleterre. Ce type d'autocar décapotable était le véhicule préféré pour les excursions.

A hundred working women leave Mile End in the East End of London to visit Hatfield House, 1925. The outing was organized by the anti-communist Mile End Unionist Association. The women were to be the guests for a day of the Marchioness of Salisbury.

Einhundert Arbeiterinnen aus Mile End im Londoner East End begeben sich auf eine Ausflugsfahrt nach Hatfield House, 1925. Der anti-kommunistische Unionistenverband von Mile End hatte die Besichtigung organisiert, bei der die Frauen einen Tag lang Gäste der Marquise von Salisbury waren.

Une centaine d'ouvrières de Mile End, dans l'est de Londres, prêtes à partir visiter Hatfield House, 1925. Une sortie organisée par le syndicat anticommuniste de Mile End. Ces femmes étaient, pour un jour, les invitées de la marquise de Salisbury.

1926. Two children race each other in a toy boat and a toy car along Deauville beach, France. Deauville was an extremely fashionable resort in the Twenties, and these children clearly come from well-off families.

1926. Zwei kleine Rennfahrer in einem Spielzeugboot und einem Spielzeugauto fahren am Strand von Deauville in Frankreich um die Wette. In den zwanziger Jahren war Deauville ein äußerst vornehmes Seebad. Diese Kinder stammen ganz offensichtlich aus wohlhabenden Familien.

1926. Deux enfants font la course, l'un dans une voiture, l'autre dans un bateau, sur la plage de Deauville, qui était très à la mode dans les années vingt. Il ne fait aucun doute que ces enfants sont issus de familles très aisées.

Members of the Royal Air Force Model Aeroplane Club, 1928. At that time, the real planes with which the RAF was equipped were little better. The race to rearm had not yet begun.

Mitglieder des Modellflugzeug-Vereins der Königlichen Luftwaffe, 1928. Zu jener Zeit waren die echten Flugzeuge der Royal Air Force kaum besser, denn das Wettrennen um die Wiederaufrüstung hatte noch nicht begonnen.

Membres du Club de modèles réduits de l'armée de l'air britannique, 1928. A cette époque, les vrais avions de la RAF. n'étaient guère plus sophistiqués que ceux-ci. La course pour le réarmement n'avait pas encore commencé.

Travelling combinations, 1928. A combined car, boat and aeroplane, possibly the prototype for *Chitty Chitty Bang Bang*, 1928.

Reisekombination, 1928. Auto, Boot und Flugzeug in einem – möglicherweise war dies der Prototyp für *Tschitti Tschitti bäng bäng*.

Voyage combiné, 1928. A la fois voiture, bateau et avion – peut-être le prototype utilisé dans *Chitty Chitty Bang Bang*.

A couple take a downriver trip on bicycle boats, 1925. The return journey would be much harder, when it was uphill all the way.

Dieses Paar unternimmt mit Tretbooten eine Fahrt flußabwärts, 1925. Der Rückweg würde sehr viel beschwerlicher werden.

Couple en balade à bord d'un pédalo, 1925. Le trajet du retour pouvait se révéler plus difficile quand il fallait pédaler à contre-courant.

W
EXTE
CLAPH

1925. The smallest racing car in the world, the *Jappic*. Driving this sort of car was more like riding a motor cycle – the driver had to throw his or her body from side to side to hold it on the road.

1925. Der kleinste Rennwagen der Welt, der *Jappic*. Um dieses Gefährt zu lenken, mußte man sich wie ein Motorradfahrer verhalten – das Gleichgewicht des Wagens mußte mit dem Körper ausbalanciert werden.

1925. La *Jappic*, plus petite voiture de course du monde. Conduire ce genre de véhicule s'apparentait davantage à la conduite d'une motocyclette – le conducteur devant se pencher d'un côté ou de l'autre pour le maintenir sur la route.

An oddity from the 1927 Motor Show. It was called the Observation Car. Passengers sat with their backs to the driver, enjoying the view through the large rear window. At least you could see what was going to run into you.

Eine Kuriosität der Automobilausstellung von 1927, der sogenannte Panoramawagen. Die Fahrgäste saßen mit dem Rücken zum Fahrer und genossen die Aussicht durch die große Heckscheibe. So konnten sie auch sehen, was bei einem Auffahrunfall auf sie zukam.

Bizarrerie du salon de l'automobile de 1927, appelée « voiture d'observation ». Tournant le dos au chauffeur, les passagers bénéficient d'une vue dégagée à l'arrière, avec l'avantage de voir venir d'éventuelles collisions.

A taxi built in the style of the old London horse-drawn hansom cab, 1925. The design did not catch on – perhaps because of steering difficulties with such a long column.

Ein Taxi im Stil der alten Londoner Hansom-Droschken, 1925. Die Konstruktion war leider kein Erfolg – vermutlich gab es Probleme beim Lenken.

Taxi conçu dans le style des anciens cabriolets londoniens, où le cocher était assis à l'arrière, 1925. Ce modèle n'a pas eu de succès – probablement parce qu'il était trop difficile à manier.

Buying on the move. A man buys his ticket at a bus stop in Paris, 1929. 'Foresight' buying, though popular in the Netherlands, France and Italy, has never been used in Britain.

Auf der Straße kaufen. Ein Mann kauft einen Fahrschein an einer Pariser Bushaltestelle, 1929. In Großbritannien wurde dieses System des Fahrscheinkaufs nie eingeführt, obwohl es auch in den Niederlanden, Frankreich und Italien beliebt war.

Acheter en marchant. Un homme achète son ticket à l'arrêt de bus, Paris, 1929. Bien que populaire aux Pays-Bas, en France et en Italie, ce système d'achat à l'avance ne fut jamais introduit en Grande-Bretagne.

Selling on the move. A 'money in the slot' automatic vending machine, 1928. The machine sold fruit and nuts and was attached to a car which presumably stopped if anyone wished to make a purchase.

Auf der Straße verkaufen. Ein Münzautomat, 1928. Der Automat diente dem Verkauf von Obst und Nüssen und war auf einen Wagen montiert, der vermutlich anhielt, sobald jemand etwas kaufen wollte.

Vendre en roulant. Distributeur automatique, 1928. Cette machine vendait des fruits frais et des noix. Elle était fixée à la voiture qui s'arrêtait probablement quand un passant désirait acheter quelque chose.

9. Sport
Sport
Le sport

The French tennis star Suzanne Lenglen in action during a doubles match at Wimbledon, June 1924. Lenglen was perhaps the greatest woman player of all time. She won the Women's Championship at Wimbledon six times in seven years during the early Twenties.

Das französische Tennis-As Suzanne Lenglen bei einem Doppel in Wimbledon, Juni 1924. Sie war die vielleich größte Tennisspielerin aller Zeiten. In den frühen zwanziger Jahren gewann sie sechsmal innerhalb von sieben Jahren das Finale der Damen in Wimbledon.

La vedette du tennis, Suzanne Lenglen, en action dans un double dames à Wimbledon, juin 1924. La Française fut l'une des plus grandes joueuses de l'histoire du tennis. Elle gagna six fois la Coupe de Wimbledon en sept ans durant des années vingt.

GAMES

9. Sport
Sport
Le sport

It was an age of heroes, of Babe Ruth on the baseball field, 'Big Bill' Tilden and Suzanne Lenglen on the tennis court, Hughie Gallagher and Charles Buchan on the football field, Steve Donaghue in the saddle, Jack Dempsey and Max Schmeling in the ring. The war was over, and it was time to salute a new kind of courage.

Sports stars made big headlines in the newspapers. The radio brought great sporting events into millions of homes – before the decade was over, you could hear live commentary on boxing, cricket, football, baseball and racing. Sport was a high-profile business, involving millions of fans and enormous sums of money – when Babe Ruth moved from the Red Sox to the New York Yankees in 1920, he demanded a salary of $20,000 a year.

The USA took the major honours at all three Olympics – Antwerp in 1920, Paris in 1924 and Amsterdam in 1928. There was still a delightful aura of real amateurism over the Games. An unknown Canadian named Percy Williams won gold medals in the 100 and 200 metres at Amsterdam after hitch-hiking across Canada to get a boat to Europe. Lord Burghley, a young English aristocrat, was the surprise winner of the 400-metre hurdles.

And, for cricket-lovers, the mild-mannered Jack Hobbs was breaking all records.

Die zwanziger Jahre waren die Zeit der Sportskanonen: Babe Ruth siegte auf dem Baseballplatz, „Big Bill" Tilden und Suzanne Lenglen auf dem Tennisplatz, Hughie Gallagher und Charles Buchan auf dem Fußballplatz, Steve Donaghue im Sattel, Jack Dempsey und Max Schmeling im Boxring. Der Krieg war vorüber, und es war an der Zeit, einer neuen Art von Mut Tribut zu zollen.

Die Sportler sorgten für Schlagzeilen. Das Radio übermittelte wichtige Sportereignisse in Millionen Wohnzimmer, und noch bevor das Jahrzehnt vorüber war, konnte man Live-

Kommentare über Boxkämpfe, Kricketmatches, Fußballspiele, Baseballbegegnungen und Autorennen im Radio mitverfolgen. Der Sport war ein profitables Geschäft, an dem Millionen von Fans und ungeheure Geldsummen beteiligt waren – als Babe Ruth 1920 von den Red Sox zu den New York Yankees wechselte, verlangte er ein Jahresgehalt von 20.000 Dollar.

Bei den drei Olympischen Spielen – in Antwerpen 1920, in Paris 1924 und in Amsterdam 1928 – gewannen die Vereinigten Staaten die meisten Medaillen. Die Olympiade hatte damals noch das Flair eines Amateurwettbewerbs. So gewann ein unbekannter Kanadier namens Percy Williams in Amsterdam die Goldmedaillen über 100 und 200 Meter, nachdem er per Anhalter quer durch Kanada gefahren war, um ein Schiff nach Europa zu erreichen. Der junge englische Aristokrat, Lord Burghley, wurde überraschend Sieger über 400 Meter Hürden.

Und für Kricketliebhaber brach der sanftmütige Jack Hobbs alle Rekorde.

Ce fut l'âge des héros : Babe Ruth sur les terrains de baseball, « Big Bill » Tilden et Suzanne Lenglen sur les courts de tennis, Hughie Gallagher et Charles Buchan sur les terrains de football, Steve Donaghue aux courses de chevaux, Jack Dempsey et Max Schmeling sur les rings de boxe. La guerre était finie : il fallait dorénavant saluer une autre forme de courage.

Les champions sportifs faisaient la une des journaux. La radio permit à des millions de foyers de suivre les grandes rencontres. A la fin des années vingt, on pouvait suivre en direct les matchs de boxe, de cricket, de football, de baseball et les courses automobiles. Le sport était un gigantesque commerce qui comptait des millions de supporters et brassait d'énormes sommes d'argent. Quand Babe Ruth quitta le club des Red Sox pour les New York Yankees en 1920, il exigea un salaire de 20 000 $ par an.

Les Etats-Unis remportèrent les plus belles médailles des trois Jeux olympiques de la décennie – Anvers en 1920, Paris en 1924 et Amsterdam en 1928. Les Jeux olympiques étaient alors une vraie célébration du sport amateur. Un Canadien inconnu, Percy Williams, gagna la médaille d'or du 100 mètres et du 200 mètres à Amsterdam. Pour cela, il lui avait d'abord fallu traverser le Canada en stop avant d'embarquer sur un bateau pour l'Europe. Lord Burghley, un jeune aristocrate anglais, remporta le 400 mètres haies, à la surprise générale.

Enfin, en cricket, il y avait Jack Hobbs, le gentleman qui battait tous les records de la discipline.

The start of a whippet race, September 1927. The dog's owner is holding it by the ear and tail, so that he can throw it into the race and give it a flying start. The sport was most popular in the North of England.

Start eines Whippet-Rennens, September 1927. Der Hundebesitzer hält den Hund bei den Ohren und dem Schwanz, damit er ihm beim Signal einen fliegenden Start ermöglichen kann. Dieser Sport war besonders im Norden Englands beliebt.

Départ d'une course de lévriers, septembre 1927. Le propriétaire tient son chien par les oreilles et la queue et le lâche au signal pour lui permettre un départ fulgurant. Ce sport était très populaire dans le nord de l'Angleterre.

Head over heels. Jockey and horse come apart during a point-to-point race on the Duke of Beaufort's estate, March 1925. Hopefully, at that time of year, the landing would have been soft.

Hals über Kopf. Pferd und Reiter straucheln bei einem Geländejagdrennen auf dem Anwesen des Herzogs von Beaufort, März 1925. Zu jener Jahreszeit war die Landung vermutlich weich.

La tête en avant. Chute d'un jockey et de son cheval lors d'une course amateurs organisée sur la propriété du duc de Beaufort, mars 1925. Espérons qu'en cette période pluvieuse de l'année, leur réception au sol ne fut pas trop dure.

Members of the Arsenal football team limber up on the pitch with a bicycle exercise, 1927. Although the exercise may seem reminiscent of a routine performed by the Alfred Jackson Dancing Girls, Arsenal were one of the crack teams of the Twenties.

Fußballspieler des Vereins Arsenal wärmen sich mit einer Radfahrübung auf, 1927. Auch wenn diese Übung fast wie eine Tanzeinlage der Alfred Jackson Dancing Girls anmutet, war das Fußballteam von Arsenal eines der besten der zwanziger Jahre.

Des joueurs de football de l'équipe de l'Arsenal pédalent en l'air pour s'échauffer, 1927. Même si l'exercice rappelle un numéro du spectacle des Alfred Jackson Dancing Girls, il s'agit bien des footballeurs de l'un des meilleurs clubs des années vingt.

Off-duty soldiers at the Tower of London play football in the snow, January 1929.

In einer Dienstpause spielen Soldaten des Tower von London im Schnee Fußball, Januar 1929.

Des soldats de la Tour de Londres, au repos, jouent au football dans la neige, janvier 1929.

The first FA Cup Final at Wembley Stadium, 28 April 1923. The ground capacity was reckoned to be 127,000, but 200,000 fought their way in. For an hour, the pitch was a seething mass of spectators. Then a single policeman on a white horse managed to impose order. Bolton beat West Ham by two goals to nil.

Das erste FA-Cup-Finale im Stadion von Wembley, 28. April 1923. Das Fassungsvermögen des Stadions schätzte man auf 127.000 Zuschauer, doch 200.000 Menschen erkämpften sich Einlaß. Eine Stunde lang bestand das Spielfeld nur aus einer wogenden Zuschauermenge, bis es einem einzelnen berittenen Polizisten gelang, für Ordnung zu sorgen. Bolton schlug West Ham mit 2 : 0 Toren.

Première finale de la coupe de la FA à Wembley, 28 avril 1923. Le stade pouvait accueillir 127 000 spectateurs, mais 200 000 personnes parvinrent à entrer. Pendant une heure, le terrain fut occupé par une masse de spectateurs en effervescence. Un policier, monté sur un cheval blanc, réussit à calmer la foule. Bolton battit West Ham par deux buts à zéro.

The Prince of Wales (riding his horse Klinlank, right) at the Melton Hunt steeplechase, 1923. The Prince later became King Edward VIII.

Der spätere König Edward VIII., damals Prinz von Wales (auf seinem Pferd Klinlank, rechts) beim Hindernisrennen der Jagd von Melton, 1923.

Le prince de Galles (sur son cheval Klinlank, à droite) participe au steeple de Melton Hunt, 1923. Le prince deviendrait le futur roi Edouard VIII.

May 1929. Henry Cotton (second from right) congratulates Walter Hagen on breaking the course record on the last hole at Muirfield, during the British Open Golf Championship. They were the two golfing giants of the Twenties.

Mai 1929. Während der offenen britischen Golfmeisterschaften gratuliert Henry Cotton (zweiter von rechts) Walter Hagen am letzten Loch des Greens von Muirfield zum neuen Platzrekord. In den zwanziger Jahren beherrschten diese beiden Männer den Golfsport.

Mai 1929. Open de golf de Grande-Bretagne. Henry Cotton (deuxième à droite) félicite Walter Hagen qui a battu le record sur le dernier trou du parcours de Muirfield. Ils étaient les deux géants du golf des années vingt.

Flying start. Drivers sprint to their cars at the start of the British Grand Prix, Belfast, 1929.

Fliegender Start. Die Fahrer sprinten zu ihren Wagen beim Start des britischen Grand-Prix-Rennens, Belfast, 1929.

Départ en flèche. Au signal de départ, les pilotes rejoignent leurs voitures en courant au Grand Prix britannique à Belfast, 1929.

Flying finish. Lord Woolavington's Captain Cuttle leads the field at the end of the Derby, Epsom, 1922. The jockey is Steve Donaghue, who gained a reputation as a brilliant but aggressive rider.

Fliegender Zieleinlauf. Am Ende des Derbys von Epsom führt Lord Woolavingtons Captain Cuttle das Feld an, 1922. Der Jockey ist Steve Donaghue, der als brillanter aber aggressiver Reiter galt.

Arrivée en trombe. Captain Cuttle, un cheval de l'écurie de lord Woolavington, mène la course au Derby d'Epsom, 1922. Le jockey est Steve Donaghue, connu pour être un cavalier génial, mais agressif.

December 1929. A car race around the oval track built on the roof of the Fiat Works in Turin. The track was there to test production cars, but Fiat already had a long history of successful motor racing.

Dezember 1929. Ein Autorennen auf dem Dach des Turiner Fiat-Werkes. Die ovale Rennstrecke war zu Testzwecken der Werksproduktion angelegt worden, denn Fiat nahm bereits seit geraumer Zeit erfolgreich an Autorennen teil.

Décembre 1929. Course sur la piste ovale construite sur les toits des usines Fiat à Turin. La piste était destinée aux essais des nouvelles voitures. Fiat avait déjà remporté un grand nombre de victoires dans le domaine de la course automobile.

FIAT

One for the pot. Mrs Eddowes prepares for a tricky billiards shot, April 1926. She was the Lyceum Club champion.

Konzentration beim Einlochen. Die Clubmeisterin des Lyceum-Club-Billardvereins, Mrs. Eddowes, bei einem schwierigen Stoß, April 1926.

Partie de billard. Mme Eddowes se prépare à exécuter un coup difficile, avril 1926. Elle était la championne du Lyceum Club.

1926. The anchor man of a tug-of-war team takes the strain during the Police Sports at the North Middlesex Ground, Hornsey. The photograph was probably taken after the General Strike, or the anchor man would have had more serious business to attend to.

1926. Den hintersten Mann trifft es beim Tauziehen am härtesten, so wie hier auf dem Polizei-Sportfest in North Middlesex, Hornsey. Diese Aufnahme entstand vermutlich nach dem Ende des Generalstreiks, sonst hätte sich der abgebildete Polizist wohl um ernstere Angelegenheiten kümmern müssen.

1926. Membre d'une équipe de tir à la corde participant au tournoi de sports de la police à Middlesex du Nord, Hornsey. Ce cliché fut certainement pris après la grève générale, sinon cet homme aurait eu des choses plus importantes à faire.

A well-balanced swing. Mr Butler, golf caddie master and mayor of Henley-on-Thames, October 1927.

Mit perfektem Schwung. Der Caddie-Meister und Bürgermeister von Henley-on-Thames, Mr. Butler, Oktober 1927.

Swing bien équilibré. M. Butler, maître caddie de golf, était aussi le maire de Henley-on-Thames, octobre 1927.

French tennis player René Lacoste on his way to defeating Mr McEwen in the Open Tennis Championships at North London Hard Courts, Highbury, April 1928.

Der französische Tennisspieler René Lacoste besiegt seinen Gegner Mr. McEwen bei den offenen Tennismeisterschaften auf den Nord-Londoner Hartplätzen von Highbury, April 1928.

Le joueur de tennis français, René Lacoste, sur le point de battre M. McEwen lors d'un tournoi de tennis se déroulant sur les courts de Highbury, au nord de Londres, avril 1928.

Safety helmets. Captain C W R Knight wears a visor as well as falconry gloves while he holds a tame golden eagle. The captain must have been a strong man – the eagle has a seven-foot wingspan and is a heavy bird.

Schutzhelme. Während Hauptmann C.W. R. Knight diesen zahmen Steinadler trägt, schützen ihn nicht nur Handschuhe sondern auch ein Visier. Da der Vogel eine Flügelspannweite von über zwei Metern und ein beachtliches Gewicht hat, muß der Hauptmann recht stark gewesen sein.

Masques de protection. Le capitaine C.W. R. Knight, équipé d'une visière et d'un gant de fauconnerie, porte un aigle royal apprivoisé. Il fallait beaucoup de forces pour porter cet oiseau qui était lourd et dont les ailes faisaient plus de deux mètres d'envergure.

November 1925. 'Hinkey' Haines from the New York Giants football team shows off the latest headgear.

November 1925. „Hinkey“ Haines vom American-Football-Team New York Giants führt die neueste Hutmode vor.

Novembre 1925. « Hinkey » Haines, joueur de l'équipe de football des New York Giants, porte un casque du dernier cri.

10. Children
Kinder
Les enfants

A group of children clamber aboard a dinghy on Brighton beach, 1928. The spirit of adventure among the young was alive and well in the Twenties.

Eine Gruppe von Kindern spielt am Strand in einem Beiboot, Brighton, 1928. Die Abenteuerlust der Jugend war in den zwanziger Jahren ungebrochen.

Des enfants à bord d'un dériveur sur la plage de Brighton, 1928. L'esprit d'aventure était bel et bien vivant chez les enfants des années vingt.

10. Children
Kinder
Les enfants

Through adult eyes, childhood always appears romantic. It may also seem deprived, horrendous, miserable, or idyllic, but is still romantic. If we believe that fiction can give an accurate portrait of an age, then childhood in the Twenties was full of adventure. The stories written for children by Richmal Crompton, Erich Kästner, A A Milne, Hergé and others suggest that children still had the freedom to wander through their immediate surroundings without having to be permanently on guard against automobiles and abusers.

The child's landscape was littered with derelict buildings, unfenced ponds, unguarded tips and slag heaps, unsprayed fields and wild, wild woods. You could swim in lakes, rivers and canals. You could shoot squirrels with improvised bows and arrows, snatch eggs from birds' nests, even steal apples from orchards without risking anything worse by way of retribution than an immediate clip round the ear from the local bobby, and a subsequent queasy stomach.

It was just as well that the great outdoors was a monumental playground. Unless you were rich, there was precious little to play with at home: a top or two, some marbles, a rag doll, and some building bricks if you were lucky. And if you were unlucky there was diphtheria, polio or scarlet fever to bring a permanent end to childhood and life itself.

Erwachsenen erscheint ihre Kindheit stets in romantischem Licht. Auch wenn sie von Entbehrungen, Schrecken, Unglück oder Idylle geprägt war, war sie dennoch stets romantisch. Wenn man glaubt, daß Dichtung die Literatur ein treues Bild zeichnen kann, dann war die Kindheit in den zwanziger Jahren voller Abenteuer. Richmal Crompton, Erich Kästner, A. A. Milne, Hergé und andere Autoren erzählen davon, daß Kinder damals noch viele Freiheiten besaßen. Sie konnten sich in ihrer unmittelbaren Umgebung frei bewegen, ohne Furcht vor dem Verkehr und Personen mit schlechten Absichten.

Der Lebensraum der Kinder war voller baufälliger Häuser, ungesicherter Teiche, unbewachter Mülldeponien und Schlackenhalden, ungespritzter Felder und unberührter Wälder. Man konnte in Seen, Flüssen und Kanälen baden. Man konnte Eichhörnchen mit improvisiertem Pfeil und Bogen schießen. Man konnte Eier aus Vogelnestern stehlen und sogar Äpfel aus Obstgärten, ohne eine schlimmere Strafe fürchten zu müssen, als vom Dorfpolizisten sofort eins hinter die Ohren und etwas später einen verdorbenen Magen zu bekommen.

Es war schon gut, daß die freie Natur ein riesiger Spielplatz war, denn wenn man nicht den höheren Kreisen angehörte, gab es nur sehr wenig, mit dem man zu Hause spielen konnte: einen oder zwei Kreisel, einige Murmeln, eine Flickenpuppe und, wenn man Glück hatte, einige Bauklötze. Oft setzten heimtückische Krankheiten wie Diphtherie, Kinderlähmung oder Scharlach der Kindheit und dem Leben ein plötzliches Ende.

Pour les adultes, l'enfance semble toujours romantique. Qu'elle ait été vécue dans la pauvreté, l'horreur la tristesse ou la joie, elle conserve malgré tout quelque chose de romantique. Si l'on estime que la littérature peut en dresser un portrait fidèle, alors l'enfance dans les années vingt fut une ère de grande aventure. A lire les contes de Richmal Crompton, Erich Kästner, A. A. Milne, Hergé et d'autres, les enfants semblaient libres d'aller et venir à leur guise, sans avoir continuellement à faire attention aux voitures ou aux personnes mal intentionnées.

Les enfants avaient pour décor des immeubles en ruines, des mares non signalées, des décharges non surveillées et des tas de feraille, des champs non traités au pesticide et des forêts sauvages. Mais il y avait aussi des lacs, des rivières et des canaux pour nager. Ils pouvaient tuer des écureuils avec leurs arcs et flèches improvisés, dérober les œufs des nids d'oiseaux et même chaparder des pommes dans les vergers environnants sans risquer grand-chose, si ce n'est une paire de gifles distribuée par le policier du village et une bonne indigestion.

Enfin, c'était tout aussi bien que le monde extérieur soit un vaste terrain de jeux car, à moins d'avoir des parents riches, on trouvait rarement des jouets à la maison : une ou deux toupies, quelques billes, une poupée de chiffon et, avec de la chance, deux ou trois plots. Pis encore, il y avait les risques de maladie : la diphtérie, la polio ou la scarlatine pouvaient handicaper et même tuer un enfant.

Play streets. Young boys playing cricket in London's East End, 1929.
In streets like these, motor cars were almost unknown, pavements made a firm playing surface, and lamp posts were excellent wickets or goal posts.

Spielstraßen. Zwei Jungen spielen Kricket im Londoner East End, 1929. In solchen Straßen waren Autos eine Seltenheit, die Bürgersteige boten einen festen Spieluntergrund, und Laternenpfähle eigneten sich hervorragend als Torpfosten.

Jeux de rue. Petits garçons jouant au cricket dans un quartier de l'est de Londres, 1929. Dans ces rues-là, les voitures étaient très rares, aussi les trottoirs faisaient-ils un bon terrain de jeu et les lampadaires d'excellents poteaux.

Aspiring boxers in Shadwell, East London, 1920. Then, as now, many saw the fight business as one of the few legitimate ways for working-class children to find fame and fortune.

Aufstrebende Boxer im Ost-Londoner Stadtteil Shadwell, 1929. Schon damals betrachtete man den Boxsport als einen der wenigen legalen Wege, auf dem Arbeiterkinder zu Ruhm und Wohlstand gelangen konnten.

Aspirants boxeurs à Shadwell, à l'est de Londres, 1920. Pour beaucoup d'enfants défavorisés, la boxe apparaissait (et apparaît encore) comme l'un des seuls moyens honnêtes pour connaître la gloire et faire fortune.

Skate-sailing in Chelsea, London, March 1929. Such a pastime would have been inconceivable a couple of generations later. Today it would be condemned as lowering the tone of the neighbourhood and adversely affecting property prices.

Rollschuh-Segeln im Londoner Stadtviertel Chelsea, März 1929. Zwei bis drei Generationen später wäre ein solcher Zeitvertreib in dieser Gegend undenkbar, da er dem Ansehen des noblen Viertels schaden und sich nachteilig auf die Grundstückspreise auswirken könnte.

Vol à voile en patins à roulettes à Chelsea, Londres, mars 1929. Un tel jeu serait impensable quelques générations plus tard. Aujourd'hui, il serait jugé peu chic et même susceptible de faire baisser la cote du quartier.

Bringing home the fireworks, 1925. In the Twenties there were no restrictions as to the minimum age at which you could buy fireworks. If you had the money, any local shopkeeper would have been happy to supply them.

Mit dem Feuerwerk nach Hause, 1925. In den zwanziger Jahren gab es keine Altersbeschränkungen für den Kauf von Feuerwerkskörpern. Wer sie bezahlen konnte, durfte sie mitnehmen, und der Händler an der Ecke war stets erfreut, seine Kunden zufriedenzustellen

Feux d'artifice pour la maison, 1925. Dans les années vingt, il n'y avait pas de restriction d'age pour acheter des feux d'artifice. Sie le client avait de l'argent, le marchand du coin était toujours ravi de satisfaire son client.

A child playing in the gutter on the streets of Berlin, 1920. 'Our favourite sport was to ride on trams without paying. And we used to nick an apple from the greengrocer's display on the way to school' – Erna Nelki.

Ein Kind spielt im Rinnstein einer Berliner Straße, 1920. „Unser Lieblingssport war das Schwarzfahren in der Straßenbahn. Und auf dem Weg zur Schule ließen wir einen Apfel aus den Auslagen des Gemüsehändlers mitgehen“, berichtet Erna Nelki.

Enfant jouant dans le caniveau d'une rue de Berlin, 1920. « Notre sport favori, c'était de voyager en tram sans payer. Puis, en passant devant l'étalage de l'épicier, sur le chemin de l'école, on volait une pomme » – Erna Nelki.

Spring-heeled. Boys playing leap-frog in a city street, England, 1929. The poet Laurie Lee wrote, 'Summer was the time of sweat running down the legs; of fights and falls and new-scabbed knees' – *Cider with Rosie*.

Spiele der Armen. Kinder beim Bockspringen in einer Straße, England, 1929. Der Dichter Laurie Lee schrieb: „Der Sommer war die Zeit, wo einem der Schweiß die Beine hinunterrann, die Zeit der Kämpfe und Stürze und frischverschorften Knie" – *Des Sommers ganze Fülle*.

Jeu de pauvres. Des garçons jouent à saute-mouton dans la rue, Angleterre, 1929. Le poète Laurie Lee écrivait : « L'été rimait avec sueur, bagarres, chutes et genoux râpés » dans *Cider With Rosie*.

Well-heeled. Eton schoolboys inspect the selection of cricket bats in Mat Wright's local shop. A good quality cricket bat would cost the equivalent of the average worker's weekly wage in the Twenties.

Spiele der Reichen. Schüler der Privatschule von Eton begutachten die Auswahl an Kricketschlaghölzern in Mat Wrights Geschäft. Ein gutes Schlagholz kostete in den zwanziger Jahren etwa den durchschnittlichen Wochenlohn eines Arbeiters.

Jeu de riches. Des élèves d'Eton examinent les différentes battes de cricket que propose le marchand du village. Dans les années vingt, le prix d'une batte de bonne qualité équivalait à peu près au salaire hebdomadaire d'un ouvrier.

Messing about by the river, 1925. As novelist George Orwell wrote, 'I wouldn't promise to go home. I wanted to stay and go fishing with the gang.'

Abenteuer am Fluß, 1925. „Ich versprach nicht, direkt nach Hause zu gehen. Ich wollte noch bleiben und mit den anderen Kindern angeln gehen", schreibt der Romancier George Orwell.

Jouer au bord de l'eau, 1925. Le romancier George Orwell écrivait : « Comment promettre de rentrer à la maison ? Je voulais rester avec mes camarades et aller à la pêche avec eux ».

Messing about on the river, 1923. Three boys compete in the annual tub race at Twickenham Children's Regatta, near London.

Abenteuer auf dem Fluß, 1923. Drei Wettstreiter beim alljährlichen Bottichrennen der Kinder-Regatta von Twickenham, in der Nähe von London.

Jouer sur l'eau, 1923. Ces trois garçons participent à la course de baignoires organisée chaque année pour les enfants de Twickenham, près de Londres.

Learning the ropes, 1920. A colliery apprentice at Ashington mine in the North of England fixes ropes to the coal tubs. 'All of us owe the decency of our lives to poor drudges underground, blackened to the eyes, with their throats full of coal dust...' – George Orwell, *The Road to Wigan Pier*.

Eine harte Schule, 1920. Ein Bergbaulehrling befestigt in der Grube von Ashington in Nordengland Kohlewaggons an einem Seil. „Jeder von uns verdankt sein anständiges Leben den hart arbeitenden Männern unter der Erde, die geschwärzt sind bis auf die Augen und deren Kehlen mit Kohlenstaub gefüllt sind ...", schreibt George Orwell in *Der Weg nach Wigan Pier*.

Apprendre les ficelles du métier, 1920. Un apprenti en train d'accrocher une chaîne à un wagonnet de charbon dans une mine d'Ashington, nord de l'Angleterre. « Nous devons notre confort à ces pauvres gamins qui triment sous terre, couverts de suie, les poumons remplis de poussière de charbon... » – George Orwell, dans *La Route qui mène au quai Wigan*.

Studying form. A young huntsman watches proceedings during the Bath Horse Show in the West of England, September 1923.

Formale Studien. Ein junger Jagdreiter verfolgt aufmerksam die Pferdeschau von Bath in Westengland, September 1923.

Apprendre l'art de l'équitation.
Un garçon en tenue de chasse assiste au concours hippique de Bath, ouest de l'Angleterre, septembre 1923.

'The Campbells are coming...' Six-year-old Donald Campbell at the wheel of a replica of his father's Bugatti at the Children's Motor Show in Selfridges, Oxford Street, London, October 1927.

„Die Campbells kommen ..." Der sechsjährige Donald Campbell steuert auf der vom Kaufhaus Selfridges organisierten Automobilausstellung für Kinder eine Nachbildung des Bugattis seines Vaters, Oxford Street, London, Oktober 1927.

« Les Campbell arrivent... » Donald Campbell, six ans, au volant d'une Bugatti, copie de celle de son père, lors d'une exposition de voitures pour enfants chez Selfridges dans la Oxford Street, Londres, octobre 1927.

Schoolboys gaze in awe at Captain Malcolm Campbell's *Bluebird*, 1929. It was the car in which, the year before, he had broken the world's land speed record on Pendine Sands in South Wales.

Einige Schuljungen bewundern ehrfürchtig Hauptmann Malcolm Campbells *Bluebird*, 1929. Mit diesem Wagen hatte er ein Jahr zuvor den Geschwindigkeitsweltrekord auf den Pendine Sands in Südwales gebrochen.

Des écoliers en admiration devant la *Bluebird* du capitaine Malcolm Campbell, 1929. C'est avec ce modèle qu'il réussit un an plus tôt à battre le record du monde de vitesse à Pendine Sands au sud du Pays de Galles.

Schoolboys' holiday. A scene that could have come from Dickens – pupils from Ardingly School in Sussex set off for their Christmas holidays, December 1926.

Schulferien. Diese Szene könnte aus einem Roman von Charles Dickens stammen. Zöglinge der Schule von Ardingly in Sussex brechen in die Weihnachtsferien auf, Dezember 1926.

Départ en vacances. Une scène que l'on pourrait croire extraite d'un roman de Dickens. Des élèves de l'école Ardingly dans le Sussex s'apprêtent à rentrer chez eux pour Noël, décembre 1926.

Busmen's holiday, August 1927. London children are unable to contain their excitement as they cram into buses for a day out. The outing was organized by the bus crews of Barking Garage.

Exkursion, August 1927. Diese Londoner Kinder können ihre Aufregung kaum verbergen, als sie sich in die Busse drängen. Den Ausflug organisierten die Angestellten der Omnibushalle von Barking.

Départ en excursion, août 1927. Des enfants de Londres, entassés dans des bus mais débordants de joie, sont prêts à partir. Cette sortie était organisée par les conducteurs de bus du garage Barking.

Hop-pickers in Kent, September 1923. Every autumn, families from the East End of London spent a week or two in the fields, stripping the ripe hops from the vines. Although it was tough work for the whole family, it was regarded as a traditional holiday.

Hopfenpflücker in Kent, September 1923. Jeden Herbst verbrachten Familien aus dem Londoner East End ein bis zwei Wochen auf den Feldern, um bei der Hopfenernte zu helfen. Trotz der harten Arbeit, empfand die ganze Familie diese Tage als Ferienzeit.

Vendangeurs dans le Kent, septembre 1923. Chaque automne, des familles de l'est de Londres passaient une semaine ou deux aux champs pour faire les vendanges. Même si toute la famille travaillait durement, c'était considéré comme des vacances.

A nanny demonstrates the noble art of nose-blowing, 1925. The teaching of etiquette began at a very young age.

Ein Kindermädchen lehrt die edle Kunst des schicklichen Schneuzens, 1925. Der Unterricht in Etikette begann schon in sehr jungen Jahren.

Une nurse montre comment faire pour se moucher noblement, 1925. L'enseignement des bonnes manières commençait dès le plus jeune âge.

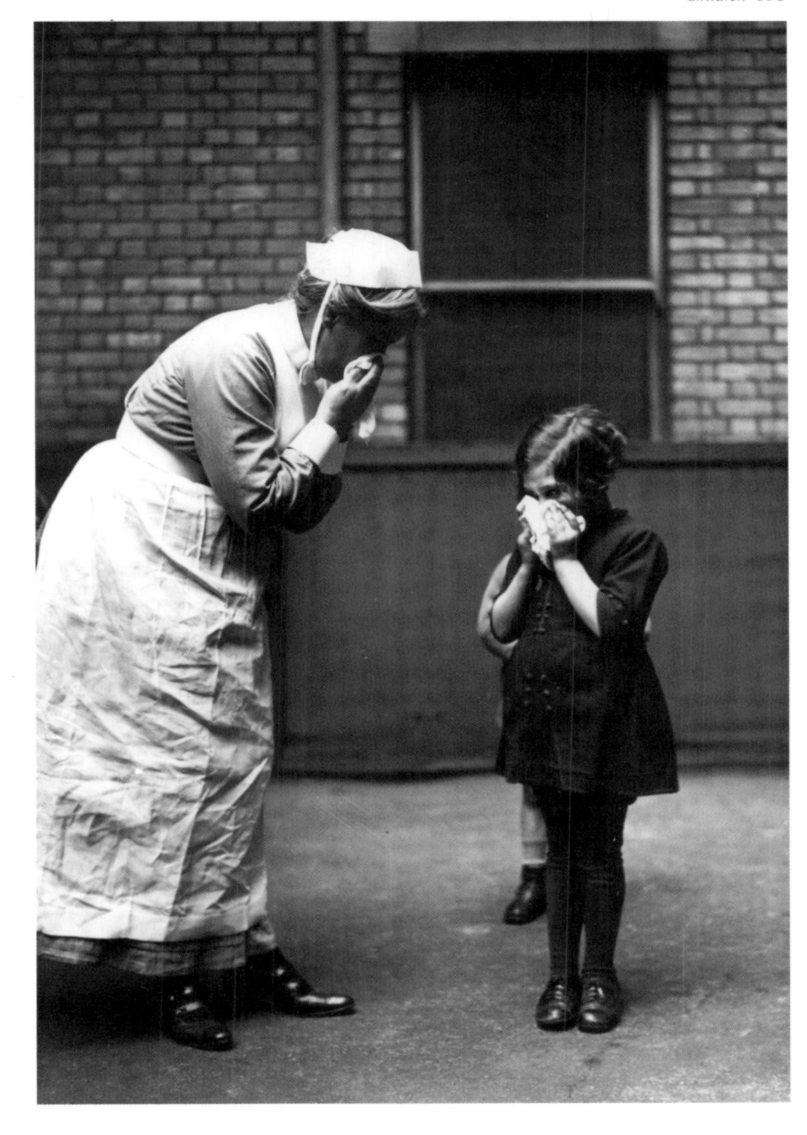

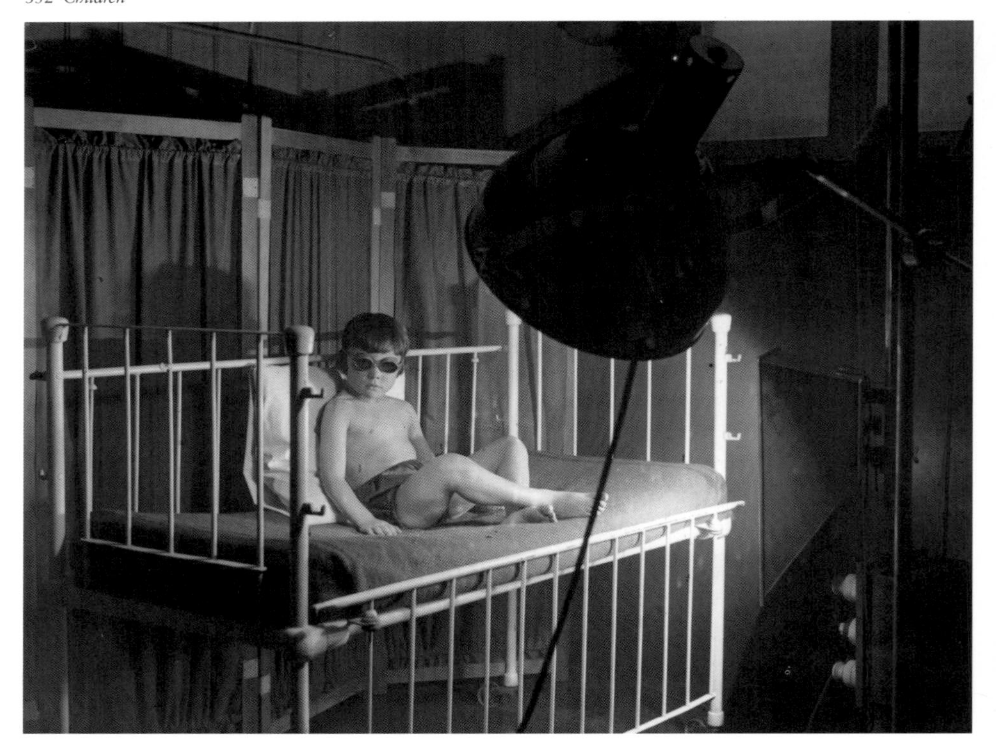

Healing rays. A child receives treatment under an artificial sun lamp, 1925. Sunlight, real or otherwise, was seen as having only health-giving properties in the Twenties. No one worried about skin cancer.

Heilende Strahlen: Ein Kind wird mit Höhensonne behandelt, 1925. Sonnenlicht, ob echt oder künstlich, schrieb man in den zwanziger Jahren ausschließlich gesundheitsfördernde Eigenschaften zu. Niemand sorgte sich zu jener Zeit um Hautkrebs.

Rayons guérisseurs. Enfant soigné à l'aide d'une lampe à ultraviolets, 1925. Dans les années vingt, le soleil, naturel ou artificiel, était considéré comme bon pour la santé. Personne ne songeait au cancer de la peau.

Informative rays. Orphans listen to a radio charity appeal, November 1925. 'For the children, nothing is too good,' wrote 'Uncle Mac', who pioneered children's broadcasting for the BBC in 1922.

Informative Wellen. Waisenkinder lauschen einem im Radio gesendeten Wohltätigkeitsaufruf, November 1925. „Für Kinder ist nichts zu schade", schrieb damals „Onkel Mac", der 1922 für die BBC auf dem Gebiet der Kindersendungen Pionierarbeit leistete.

Ondes pédagogiques. Orphelins écoutant un programme de charité à la radio, novembre 1925. « Pour les enfants, rien n'est trop bon », écrivait l'« Oncle Mac » qui créa en 1922 les premières émissions pour enfants de la BBC.

Swimming drill in the school playground, 1923. In those days, teachers felt they would lose dignity if they joined in. Maybe today they have no dignity left to lose.

Schwimmübungen auf dem Schulhof, 1923. Zu jener Zeit beteiligten sich Lehrer nicht an den sportlichen Übungen, weil sie fürchteten, dabei ihre Würde zu verlieren. Heute besitzen sie vermutlich keine Würde mehr, die sie verlieren könnten.

Exercices de natation dans la cour d'une école, 1923. A cette époque, les instituteurs craignaient de perdre leur dignité en prenant part à ces exercices. Aujourd'hui, il n'ont peut-être plus de dignité à perdre.

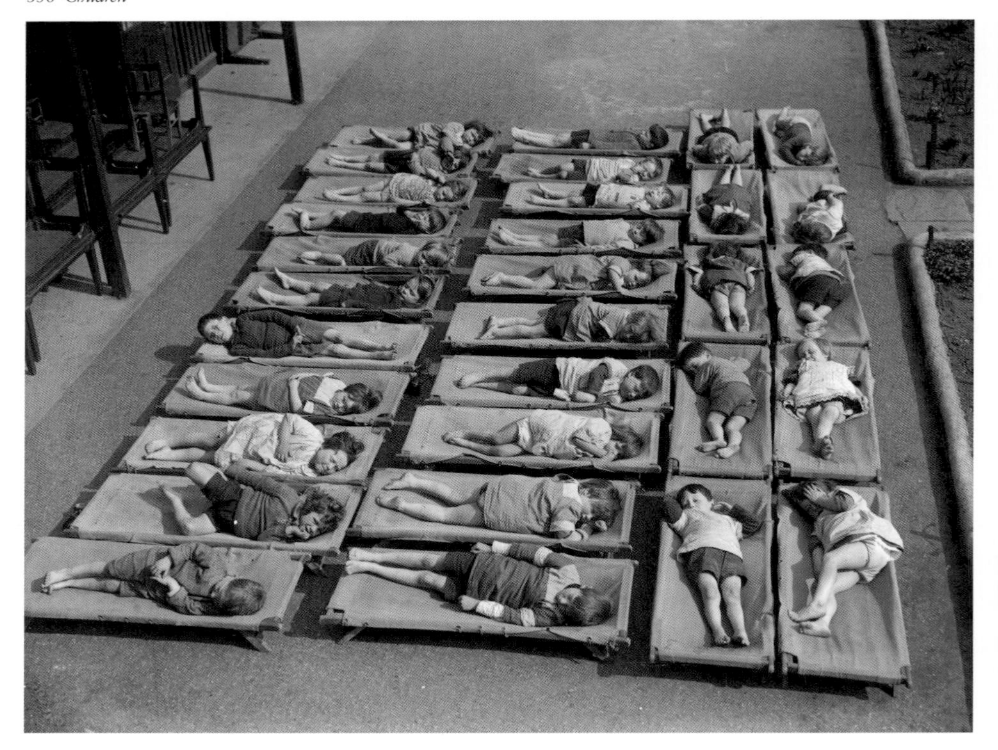

Open air schools, 1927 (above and right). Children at the Rachel McMillan Home in London have a midday nap on camp beds. Rachel and her sister Margaret devoted their lives to improving school provision for very young children.

Freiluftschulen, 1927 (oben und rechts). Zöglinge des Londoner Kinderheims von Rachel McMillan halten ihren Mittagsschlaf im Freien. Rachel und ihre Schwester Margaret hatten sich zum Ziel gesetzt, die schulische Versorgung kindgerechter zu gestalten.

Ecoles en plein air, 1927 (ci-dessus et à droite). Les enfants du foyer Rachel McMillan à Londres font leur sieste sur des lits de camp. Rachel et sa sœur Margaret ont consacré leur vie à améliorer l'école pour les enfants en bas âge.

Smart hair. Page boys at the Hotel Cecil, London, prepare for an inspection, May 1929. The Cecil was one of the largest hotels in the West End.

Eine gepflegte Frisur. Zwei Pagen im Londoner Hotel Cecil bereiten sich auf eine Inspektion vor, Mai 1929. Das Cecil war eines der größten Hotels im West End.

Bien coiffés. Des grooms de l'hôtel Cecil à Londres se préparent pour l'inspection, mai 1929. Le Cecil était l'un des plus grands hôtels du West End à Londres.

Fresh air. A group of children from a London hospital sit on the beach, July 1929. According to poet Laurie Lee, 'In those days young children dropped dead like chickens... at least a quarter were not expected to survive.'

Frische Luft. Kinder aus einem Londoner Krankenhaus sitzen am Strand, Juli 1929. „In jenen Tagen fielen kleine Kinder um wie die Fliegen ... man konnte davon ausgehen, daß wenigstens ein Viertel von ihnen nicht überleben würde", schreibt Laurie Lee.

Au grand air. Des enfants d'un hôpital de Londres à la plage, juillet 1929. Selon le poète Laurie Lee : « En ces temps-là, les enfants en bas âge mouraient comme des mouches... on estimait que près d'un quart d'entre eux ne survivrait pas ».

Middle-class domestic peace and calm, November 1922. In the Twenties, the contrast between the homes of the 'haves' and 'have-nots' was staggering.

Der häusliche Frieden der Mittelschicht, November 1922. In den zwanziger Jahren war der Unterschied zwischen den Heimen der Wohlhabenden und den Unterkünften der Mittellosen schlichtweg atemberaubend.

Paix et calme dans un foyer de la classe moyenne, novembre 1922. Dans les années vingt, le contraste entre les maisons des nantis et celles des démunis était effrayant.

A hoop-bowling race in Hyde Park, London, 1922. The picture could have been taken almost anywhere, but the clothes worn by parent and child indicate that a comfortable and well-provided home is not far away.

Ein Reifen-Rennen im Hyde Park, London, 1922. Diese Aufnahme hätte überall entstehen können, aber die Kleidung der Eltern und des Kindes läßt auf eine gute Adresse in unmittelbarer Nähe des Parks schließen.

Course de cerceaux à Hyde Park, Londres, 1922. Ce cliché aurait pu être pris à peu près n'importe où. Seuls les vêtements que portent le père et les enfants révèlent qu'ils habitent non loin de là, dans une maison confortable et bien équipée.

Plaything for the palace, 1925. The infant Maharajah of Jodhpur plays with a toy house.

Ein Spielzeug für den Palast, 1925. Der junge Maharadscha von Jodhpur vergnügt sich mit einem Spielzeughaus.

Jouet au palais, 1925. Le très jeune maharajah de Jodhpur jouant avec une petite maison.

A palace plaything, 1923. Queen Mary's dolls' house is packed, ready to be delivered to Windsor Castle. The house was designed by the architect Sir Edwin Lutyens, and was a present to the Queen.

Ein Palast zum Spielen, 1923. Queen Marys Puppenhaus wird verpackt, um nach Schloß Windsor geliefert zu werden. Das Haus hatte der Architekt Sir Edwin Lutyens entworfen, und es war ein Geschenk für die Königin.

Un palais pour jouer, 1923. Emballage de la maison de poupées devant être livrée à la reine Mary, au château de Windsor. Cette maison, dessinée par l'architecte sir Edwin Lutyens, était un cadeau à la reine.

Pupils at the Bluecoat School, Liverpool, are taught the recipe for Christmas pudding, 1925. The likelihood was that some of them came from families that could not afford the ingredients.

Schülerinnen der Bluecoat-Schule in Liverpool lernen die richtige Zubereitung eines Plumpuddings, 1925. Wahrscheinlich stammten einige der Zöglinge aus Familien, die sich nicht einmal die Zutaten leisten konnten.

Des élèves de l'école Bluecoat à Liverpool apprennent la recette du Christmas pudding, 1925. Parmi ces élèves, certains viennent probablement de familles n'ayant pas même les moyens d'acheter les ingrédients nécessaires à sa préparation.

Apprentice chefs carry an enormous Christmas pudding into the dining room of the Berkeley Hotel, London, December 1928.

Nachwuchsköche tragen einen gewaltigen Plumpudding in den Speisesaal des Londoner Berkeley Hotels, Dezember 1928.

Ces apprentis cuisiniers portent un Christmas pudding enorme jusqu'à la salle à manger de l'hôtel Berkeley à Londres, décembre 1928.

Late summer joys. Father and child cool their feet in Regent's Park, London, September 1929. Some summers in the Twenties were so hot and so dry that guns were fired at clouds in an attempt to precipitate rain.

Ein spätsommerliches Vergnügen. Vater und Kind erfrischen sich mit einem Fußbad im Londoner Regent's Park, September 1929. Die Sommer waren in den zwanziger Jahren mitunter so heiß und trocken, daß man mit Gewehren in die Wolken schoß, um Niederschläge auszulösen.

Joies d'un été indien. Père et enfant prennent un bain de pieds à Regent's Park, Londres, septembre 1929. Dans les années vingt, il y eut plusieurs étés où il fit si chaud et sec, que l'on tira des coups de feu dans le ciel, dans l'espoir de faire tomber la pluie.

A group of London children listen to the reminiscences of 'Old Tom' of Lambeth, January 1929. Nowadays, Old Tom would find it hard to gather such an audience, and might well find himself regarded as a suspicious character.

Londoner Kinder lauschen den Erinnerungen des „Alten Tom" im Stadtteil Lambeth, Januar 1929. Heutzutage würde es dem alten Mann sicher schwerfallen, ein solches Publikum um sich zu scharen, denn man würde ihm vermutlich mit erheblichem Mißtrauen begegnen.

Un groupe d'enfants de Londres écoute les souvenirs du « vieux Tom » de Lambeth, janvier 1929. De nos jours, ce vieux Tom aurait bien de la peine à réunir un tel auditoire sans susciter quelque méfiance.

11. All human life
Menschliches, Allzumenschliches
Petits et grands événements de la vie

1925. A terrifying demonstration of the alloy-metal helmet and breastplate recommended for the German police. Hopefully, not everyone who wore the protective outfit turned into Frankenstein's monster.

1925. Eine furchteinflößende Demonstration eines Metall-Kopfschutzes und Brustpanzers, die deutschen Polizisten empfohlen wurde. Es blieb zu hoffen, daß nicht jeder, der diese Schutzkleidung trug, sich in Frankensteins Monster verwandeln würde.

1925. Frissons pendant la démonstration du casque en métal et du plastron recommandés à la police allemande. Espérons que, contrairement à ce personnage, les personnes dotées d'un pareil équipement ne se transformeraient pas en monstre de Frankenstein.

11. All human life
Menschliches, Allzumenschliches
Petits et grands événements de la vie

The Twenties burst into people's lives as no other age had ever done. Before the decade was a year old there was jazz everywhere, communism and civil war in Russia, short skirts in every town and city, fighting on the streets in Berlin, a coup in Hungary, the Dada movement, revolution in Mexico, votes for women, the partition of Ireland, and a bomb blast on Wall Street.

People took to this new world of frenetic and feverish excitement with manic enthusiasm. After the suffering and slaughter of World War I they were prepared to believe in anything that promised a good time. 'What'll we do with ourselves this afternoon?' cries Daisy, one of the characters in F Scott Fitzgerald's *The Great Gatsby* – 'and the day after that and the next thirty years?'

There was always plenty to do – invent a new dance; try a new stunt; go higher, faster, further than anyone had ever gone before. Sit on a pole, jump on a pogo stick, leap into a car and tear off into the future. The important thing was to be doing *something*, and if it brought in a buck or two, so much the better.

Die zwanziger Jahre begannen mit einem so gewaltigen Paukenschlag wie kein anderes Jahrzehnt zuvor. Bereits das erste Jahr sorgte für viel Wirbel: Überall hörte man Jazzmusik, in Rußland herrschten Kommunismus und Bürgerkrieg, in der Mode setzten sich die kurzen Röcke durch. In Berlin tobten Straßenkämpfe, in Ungarn gabes einien Staatsstreich. In der Kunst kam der Dadaismus auf. Es gab eine Revolution in Mexiko. Das Wahlrecht für Frauen wurde eingeführt und die Teilung Irlands beschlossen, und auf der Wall Street explodierte eine Bombe.

Die Menschen stürzten sich in geradezu fieberhafter Begeisterung in diese neue, stürmische

Welt. Nach den Entbehrungen und dem Blutvergießen des Ersten Weltkrieges waren sie bereit, an alles zu glauben, was ihnen Freude versprach. „Was machen wir bloß heute nachmittag?" fragt Daisy, eine der Figuren in Scott F. Fitzgeralds *Der große Gatsby*. „Und was morgen, und was in den nächsten 30 Jahren?"

Es gab so viele Dinge zu tun – man konnte einen neuen Tanz erfinden, ein neues Kunststück probieren, neue Rekorde – höher, schneller, weiter – aufstellen oder sich einfach auf einen Pfahl setzen, mit einem Springseil hüpfen, in einen Wagen springen und in die Zukunft rasen. Das wichtigste war, *überhaupt* etwas zu tun, und wenn es außerdem noch etwas Geld einbrachte, um so besser.

La période des années vingt changea la vie des gens comme aucune époque auparavant. La décennie était à peine entamée qu'il y avait déjà le jazz omniprésent, le communisme et la guerre civile en Russie, des robes courtes en ville et à la campagne, des affrontements dans les rues de Berlin, un coup d'Etat en Hongrie, le mouvement dada, la révolution au Mexique, le droit de vote pour les femmes dans certains pays, l'Irlande qui se divisait en deux et une bombe qui explosait à Wall Street.

Les gens s'enthousiasmèrent pour ce monde nouveau, frénétique et agité. Après les souffrances et les massacres de la Première Guerre mondiale, ils étaient prêts à croire à tout ce qui était synonyme de plaisir. « Qu'allons-nous faire cet après-midi ? » demande Daisy, l'un des personnages de F. Scott Fitzgerald dans *Gatsby le magnifique*, « et que ferons-nous demain et pendant les 30 prochaines années ? »

Et il y avait tant de choses à faire – inventer une nouvelle danse, tenter une nouvelle acrobatie, voler plus haut, rouler plus vite, aller plus loin que jamais personne auparavant. Rester assis au sommet d'un mât, sauter avec des échasses ou grimper dans une voiture et filer à toute allure vers le futur. L'important, c'était de faire *quelque chose* et si cela rapportait quelques sous, c'était encore mieux.

Lillian Boyer, stunt-flying acrobat, January 1922. Women took to the sky in swarms. Laura Bromwell was killed when she lost control of her plane while looping the loop. Ruth Elder almost made it across the Atlantic in 1927. A year later, Amelia Earhart successfully crossed from Boston to South Wales.

Die Kunstflugakrobatin Lillian Boyer, Januar 1922. Der Himmel hatte zu jener Zeit eine geradezu magische Anziehungskraft auf Frauen. Laura Bromwell kam ums Leben, als sie bei einem Looping die Kontrolle über ihr Flugzeug verlor. Ruth Elder gelang im Jahre 1927 um ein Haar die Überquerung des Atlantischen Ozeans. Und im darauffolgenden Jahr flog schließlich Amelia Earhart erfolgreich von Boston nach Südwales.

Lillian Boyer, cascadeuse, janvier 1922. Les femmes se passionnèrent pour l'aviation. Laura Bromwell fut tuée, après avoir tenté un looping et perdu le contrôle de son avion. Ruth Elder rata de peu la traversée de l'Atlantique en 1927, mais, un an plus tard, Amelia Earhart vola de Boston au pays de Galles avec succès.

Harry Gardiner (of Washington DC) hangs from the 24th storey of the McAlpine Hotel, Broadway, New York, 1925.

Harry Gardiner (aus Washington, D. C.) hängt an der Dachkante des 24. Stockwerks des McAlpine Hotels am Broadway, New York, 1925.

Harry Gardiner (de Washington D. C.) suspendu au 24e étage de l'hôtel McAlpine à Broadway, New York, 1925.

Strange headgear. Two members of the Earls Court Circus, London, 1928. Hopefully, both of them got some enjoyment out of this particular trick.

Eine merkwürdige Kopfbedeckung. Zwei Angehörige des Earls Court Circus, London, 1928. Hoffentlich bereitete dieses besondere Kunststück nicht nur einem von beiden Vergnügen.

Etrange couvre-chef. Deux membres du cirque d'Earls Court, Londres, 1928. Espérons que le dompteur comme l'éléphant prenaient plaisir à exécuter ce numéro très particulier.

Strange clothes. An attendant at a snake farm in Port Elizabeth, South Africa, covers himself in pythons, 1928.

Eine merkwürdige Bekleidung. Ein Wärter auf einer Schlangenfarm in Port Elizabeth, Südafrika, bedeckt seinen Körper mit Pythonschlangen, 1928.

Etrange habit. Un gardien d'un élevage de serpents s'est couvert de pythons, Port Elizabeth, Afrique du Sud, 1928.

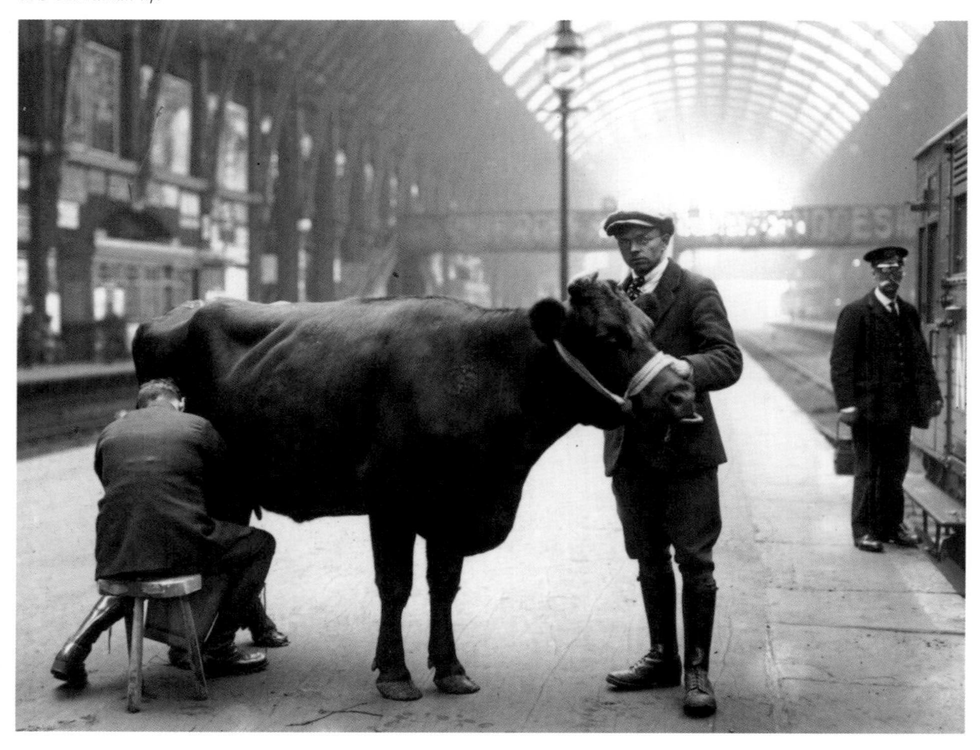

London, 1926. A cow is milked on a platform at King's Cross Station. The location for milking may not be as silly as it sounds – it might have been easier to bring a single cow than many churns of milk to the city during the General Strike.

London, 1926. Auf einem Bahnsteig des Bahnhofs King's Cross wird eine Kuh gemolken. Die Angelegenheit war wohl nicht so außergewöhnlich, denn während des Generalstreiks war es einfacher, eine Kuh als die zahlreichen Milchkannen in die Stadt zu bringen.

Londres, 1926. Récolte de lait sur le quai de la gare de King's Cross. Traire une vache en ces lieux n'est pas aussi idiot qu'il y paraît. Il est possible que, durant la grève générale, il ait été plus facile de transporter une vache que des bidons de lait.

The charge of the furry brigade, Ampthill House llama farm, 1926. Few people thought of animal rights in the Twenties, and maybe the llamas enjoyed the ride.

Die Last der Fellbrigade auf der Lama-Farm von Ampthill House, 1926. In den zwanziger Jahren waren Tierschutzvereine noch unbekannt, aber vielleicht gefiel den Lamas dieser Ausritt sogar.

Brigade au pas de charge. Elevage de lamas à Ampthill House, 1926. A cette époque, peu de gens se préoccupaient des droits des animaux. Quant aux lamas, peut-être aimaient-il se promener ainsi.

Rambling Gold breaks the canine high jump record, December 1925. He cleared 12 feet (3.6 metres), watched by his owner, John Drake.

Rambling Gold bricht den Hochsprungrekord für Hunde, Dezember 1925. In Begleitung seines Besitzers, John Drake, übersprang er die enorme Höhe von 3,60 Metern.

Rambling Gold, gagnant du concours de saut en hauteur pour chiens, décembre 1925. Il accomplit un saut de 3,6 mètres de haut, sous le regard de son propriétaire, John Drake.

If all else failed in 1927, you could always try to make a fortune with the aid of a tightrope-walking goat. At least its wild ancestors would have been used to heights.

Wenn alle Pläne fehlschlugen, konnte man 1927 immer noch versuchen, mit Hilfe einer seiltanzenden Ziege ein Vermögen zu verdienen. Zumindest deren wilde Vorfahren waren mit Sicherheit schwindelfrei.

En 1927, quand tout le reste avait échoué, on pouvait toujours tenter de faire fortune avec ce bouc-funambule. Du moins les ancêtres de l'animal devaient-ils être habitués aux hauteurs.

Crazy days, crazy ways. Theatres were prepared to snap up any novelty act in the Twenties, including the Polish giant supporting a motordrome and two motorcyclists on his chest, USA, 1928.

Ideen muß man haben. Die Varietétheater der zwanziger Jahre waren für jede Sensation dankbar – auch für diesen polnischen Hünen, der ein Motodrom und zwei Motorradfahrer auf seiner Brust balanciert, USA, 1928.

Années folles, jeux fous. Les théâtres étaient prêts à accueillir tous les numéros possibles et imaginables, comme celui du géant polonais capable de soutenir avec son buste un mini-vélodrome et deux motocyclistes, Etats-Unis, 1928.

Ben Darwin pulls a seven-passenger saloon car by his hair, USA, 1925. Of course, his hair was a perfect mess for days afterwards, but it was a living.

Ben Darwin zieht eine mit sieben Personen besetzte Limousine an seinen Haaren über die Straße, USA, 1925. Seine Frisur sah zwar anschließend tagelang katastrophal aus, aber er bestritt so immerhin seinen Lebensunterhalt.

Ben Darwin tire avec ses cheveux une limousine contenant sept passagers, Etats-Unis, 1925. On n'ose pas imaginer l'état de sa chevelure les jours suivants, mais enfin c'était une manière de gagner son pain.

Not a scientific wonder, but simply a piece of fancy-dress fun, 1925. If lucky, you picked up your local radio station. If unlucky, you electrocuted yourself.

Kein Wunder der Wissenschaft, sondern lediglich ein Spaß für einen Kostümball, 1925. Glück oder Unglück. Entweder Sie haben Ihre eigene lokale Radiostation, oder aber Sie werden durch einen Stromschlag getötet.

Ce n'est pas un miracle scientifique mais un simple déguisement. Avec de la chance vous captiez votre station de radio locale. Avec malchance vous vous électrocutiez.

Pope Pius XI and other dignitaries of the Catholic church gather for the opening of Vatican Radio, 1929. Pius also ended the 59-year-old custom of his predecessors not to leave the Vatican, under any circumstances.

Papst Pius XI. und andere Würdenträger der katholischen Kirche versammeln sich zur Eröffnung des hauseigenen Radiosenders des Vatikans, 1929. Pius XI brach auch mit der 59 Jahre alten Sitte seiner Vorgänger, den Vatikan unter keinen Umständen je zu verlassen.

Le pape Pie XI et d'autres dignitaires de l'Eglise catholique réunis pour l'inauguration de Radio Vatican, 1929. Pie XI mit ainsi fin à une tradition de ses prédécesseurs, vieille de 59 ans, interdisant au pape de quitter le Vatican, quelles que soient les circonstances.

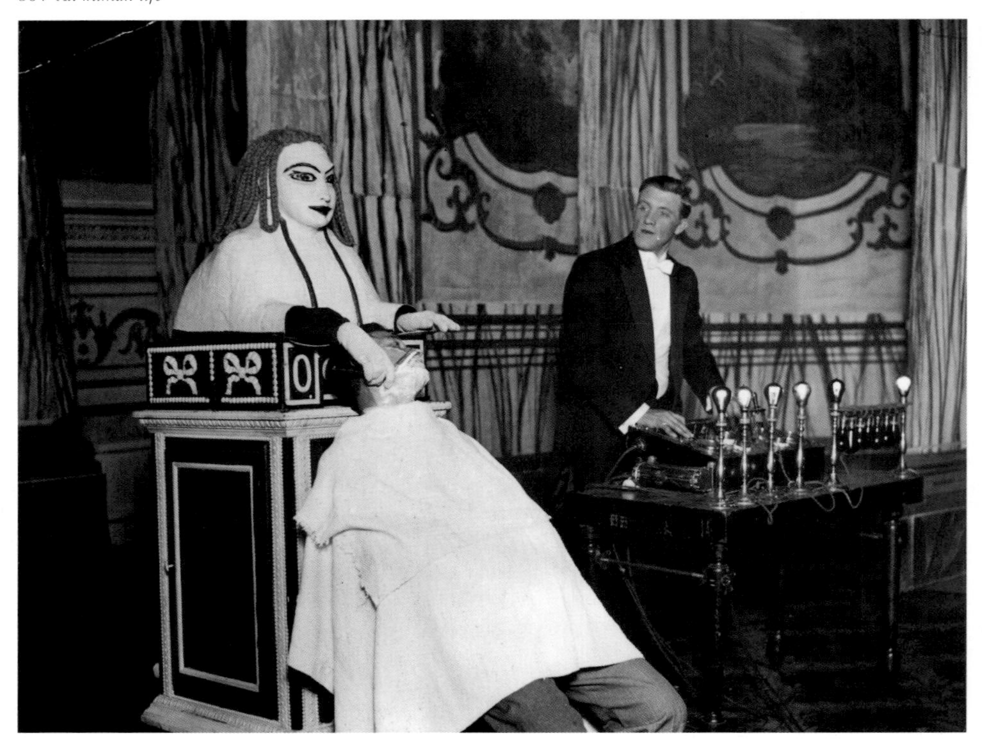

Professor Popjie demonstrates his wondrous invention, 'Radiana', 1925. Radiana was a pair of mechanical hands, containing human bones, which the Professor claimed could respond to electricity. Here Radiana is shaving a human guinea pig. There is no follow-up picture.

Professor Popjie stellt seine wundersame Erfindung „Radiana" vor, 1925. Radiana verfügte über mechanische Hände mit menschlichen Knochen, die dem Professor zufolge auf elektrische Reize reagierten. Auf dieser Aufnahme rasiert Radiana eine wagemutige Versuchsperson. Vom Ausgang des Experiments ist leider nichts bekannt.

Le professeur Popjie présente son étonnante invention, « Radiana », 1925. Il affirmait que les deux mains mécaniques de Radiana, conçues avec des os humains, fonctionnaient à l'électricité. Ici, Radiana rase un volontaire. Il n'existe aucun cliché pour témoigner du résultat.

An apparently armless man displays his ability to type with his toes, 1920. Again, this is part of a stage act. The piano to the side of the stage suggests that the encore would be even more exciting.

Ein Mann ohne Arme schreibt mit den Zehen Schreibmaschine, 1920. Selbstverständlich ist dies Teil einer Vorführung. Das Klavier, das linker Hand auf der Bühne steht, läßt eine noch interessantere Zugabe erwarten.

Un homme apparemment dépourvu de bras tape à la machine avec ses orteils, 1920. Bien entendu, ceci fait partie d'un spectacle. Le piano installé sur la scène permet de penser que les rappels seraient encore plus animés.

A partygoer at the New Year's Day Dance at the Olympic Hall, 1924.

Ein Partygast beim Neujahrs-Tanzball in der Olympic Hall, 1924.

Invité au bal du nouvel an donné à l'Olympic Hall, 1924.

August 1927. Three entries for the marrow class at the Railwaymen's Horticultural Show. The expression on the competitor's face is proof that gardening, at least, should be taken seriously in the otherwise frivolous Twenties.

August 1927. Drei Meldungen für den Wettbewerb in der Gartenkürbis-Klasse auf der Gartenbauausstellung der Eisenbahner. Der Gesichtsausdruck des Teilnehmers beweist, daß in den sonst so frivolen zwanziger Jahren zumindest die Gartenarbeit ernst genommen werden sollte.

Août 1927. Trois courges présentées au Concours d'horticulture des cheminots. A voir l'expression du participant, il ne fait pas de doute que le jardinage était une activité très sérieuse, peu en phase avec l'esprit frivole des années vingt.

Lady members of the Trail Riders use their less-than-ten-gallon hats for drinking purposes, 1926. They were hiking across the Canadian Rockies.

Weibliche Trail Riders verwenden ihre riesigen Hüte als Trinkgefäße, 1926. Sie waren gerade auf dem Weg durch die kanadischen Rocky Mountains.

Des femmes membres d'un club de randonnée se servent de leurs larges chapeaux pour se désaltérer, 1926. Elles participaient à une randonnée à travers les montagnes Rocheuses du Canada.

February 1926. Pancake Day at Olney, England. The pancake race originated in 1445, but was revived in 1925 by Mr Barratt, the sexton. He told the local young women that when the bell rang, they had to make a pancake, run to the church and exchange it for a kiss. They believed him.

Februar 1926. Fastnachtsdienstag in der englischen Stadt Olney. Das traditionelle Pfannkuchen-Rennen, das auf das Jahr 1445 zurückgeht, wurde 1925 von dem Küster Mr. Barratt leicht abgewandelt. Er erklärte den ortsansässigen jungen Frauen, daß sie, sobald die Kirchenglocke ertöne, einen Pfannkuchen backen, ihn schnellstens zur Kirche bringen und gegen einen Kuß eintauschen müßten. Sie glaubten ihm.

Février 1926. Fête de la Chandeleur à Olney, Angleterre. La course des crêpes créée en 1445 fut rétablie en 1925 par M. Barratt, le sacristain. Il raconta aux jeunes filles du village qu'elles devaient faire une crêpe au premier son de cloche. puis courir à l'église et donner leur crêpe en échange d'un baiser. Elles crurent à son histoire.

Scottish herring-gutters take a breather on a mountain of barrels, Great Yarmouth, on the east coast of England, 1925. The women travelled down for the herring harvest each year.

Schottische „Heringsmädchen" entspannen sich auf aufgestapelten Fischfässern in Great Yarmouth an der Ostküste Englands, 1925. Jedes Jahr reisten sie hierher, um in der Heringssaison bei der Verarbeitung der Fische zu helfen.

Des videuses de harengs prennent un bol d'air frais sur une montagne de fûts à Great Yarmouth, côte est de l'Angleterre, 1925. Elles étaient Ecossaises et descendaient chaque année pour l'ouverture de la saison de pêche.

People fish for bottles of wine at a Paris fairground, 1925. The game was the latest craze to hit France. It called for a steady hand, so there were few winners of more than one bottle.

Besucher eines Pariser Jahrmarkts angeln nach Weinflaschen, 1925. Dieses Geduldsspiel war in Frankreich der letzte Schrei. Da es eine ruhige Hand erforderte, kam es äußerst selten vor, daß jemand mehr als eine Flasche gewann.

Pêche miraculeuse à la foire de Paris, 1925. Ce jeu était très en vogue en France. Il fallait être habile aussi, rares étaient ceux qui gagnaient plus d'une bouteille.

Cornwall, 1926. The Port Isaac lifeboat scrapes through the streets on the way to its first launch. It may have arrived at the village by train and road. It would have been easier if it had come by sea.

Cornwall, 1926. Das Rettungsboot von Port Isaac wird auf dem Weg zu seinem Stapellauf durch die engen Dorfgassen gezwängt. Vermutlich gelang es per Eisenbahn- und Straßentransport nach Port Isaac. Ein Transport zur See wäre erheblich einfacher gewesen.

Cornouailles, 1926. Ce bateau de sauvetage, de Port Isaac, a de la peine à gagner son nouveau port d'attache. Il aurait été plus simple de le transporter par la mer au lieu d'utiliser le train et la route.

Index

How to buy or license a picture from this book

The pictures in this book are drawn from the extensive archives of The Hulton Getty Picture Collection, originally formed in 1947 as the Hulton Press Library. The Collection contains approximately 15 million images, some of which date from the earliest days of photography. It includes original material from leading press agencies – Topical Press, Keystone, Central Press, Fox Photos and General Photographic Agency as well as from *Picture Post*, the *Daily Express* and the *Evening Standard*.

Picture Licensing Information

To license the pictures listed below please call Getty Images **+ 44 171 266 2662** or email **info@getty-images.com** your picture selection with the page/reference numbers.

Hulton Getty Online

All of the pictures listed below and countless others are available via Hulton Getty Online at: **http://www.hultongetty.com**

Buying a print

For details of how to purchase exhibition-quality prints call The Hulton Getty Picture Gallery **+ 44 171 376 4525**